Supplier Selection

Judith A. Stimson

PT Publications, Inc.
3109 45th Street, Suite 100
West Palm Beach, FL 33407-1915
(561) 687-0455

Library of Congress Cataloging in Publication Data

Stimson, Judith A.
    Supplier selection / Judith A. Stimson.
        p.   cm.
    Includes bibliographical references and index.
    ISBN 0-945456-32--8
    1. Industrial procurement--Management.   I. Title.
HD39.5.S75 1998   97-38467
658.7'22--dc21   CIP

TABLE OF CONTENTS

About the Author

Judith A. Stimson has over six years management consulting experience with Global 1000 firms. She is currently an Associate Partner with Andersen Consulting, and was previously a Principal with Gemini Consulting. Some of her clients include: Frito-Lay, Earthgrains, Ocean Spray, Samsung Electronics, Stella Foods, General Mills, Kmart, Bausch & Lomb, Reckitt & Colman, National Convenience Stores, Heinz, Novacor Chemicals, DuPont/Conoco, and Philip Morris. Her industry experience includes over twelve years at Procter & Gamble in multiple procurement and manufacturing management positions.

Ms. Stimson holds a Masters of Business Administration in Finance from Xavier University and a Bachelor of Science in Management from The Pennsylvania State University where she graduated first in her class. Her certifications include APICS (CIRM and CPIM), NAPM (C.P.M.), and IMC (CMC). She has also published several articles, and been a speaker at international conferences including APICS' 1994 International Conference & Exhibition in San Diego, California; NZPICS' 1995 World Symposium of Integrated Resource Management in Auckland, New Zealand; and GMA's 1997 Invoice Accuracy Seminar in Chicago, Illinois.

In addition to the American Production & Inventory Control Society (APICS), National Association of Purchasing Management (NAPM), and Institute of Management Consultants (IMC), Ms. Stimson is also currently a member of the Council of Logistics Management (CLM), Academy of Management (AOM), and American Society for Training & Development (ASTD).

Ms. Stimson has taught approximately twenty industrial purchasing, economics, and other business courses at the Raymond Walters College of the University of Cincinnati. She currently serves on the Board of Directors of Junior Achievement in Tampa, Florida, and the Alumni Advisory Assessment Board of the Department of Management and Organization in The Smeal College of Business Administration at The Pennsylvania State University.

The views and opinions expressed in this book are those of the author and do not necessarily reflect the official policies or opinions of her organization.

How to Use This Book

This book is designed to be used in conjunction with the corollary texts in our Purchasing Series. Please call us at the number below for more information about utilizing our tools. The idea behind this book is to read it with a pen in your hand so that you can answer the questions and write down the plans you are going to put into action. For those people who use this book alone, there is enough information to get you started on the road to excellence. Remember, however, that roadmaps such as this book are best accompanied by travel guides such as the ones we offer in the field of purchasing. Together, they can make your journey a rewarding one.

HELP DESK HOTLINE
1-800-547-4326

In order to answer the questions of our readers, we have established a Help Desk Hotline at our corporate head-quarters in West Palm Beach, Florida. We invite you to call us with your queries about how to use the forms and tools in this book.

We also invite you to use our HELP DESK HOTLINE to find out more about other books we publish, as well as our *Supplier Surveys and Audits Forms* software and a videotape series entitled **Supplier Certification: The Path to Excellence**. In addition to books, software and videotapes, we offer over 80 courses which can be scheduled for intensive, in-house seminars. Call us for details.

What is Supplier Selection?

In order to describe supplier selection and grasp its significance, it is important to understand some definitions first, including:

- **Procure** - "to get by care or effort; obtain; secure; to bring about; cause"

- **Purchase** - "to get by paying a price; buy; to get in return for something"

- **Selection** - "the act of choosing; choice; a quantity or variety to choose from"

- **Supplier** - "a person or thing that supplies; provider; purveyor"

This book is about using care and effort (procuring) to choose (select) from alternative providers (suppliers) of materials and services. While often looked at as a means to reducing costs, sourcing can be a bigger lever than enhancing revenue efforts (for example, sales growth) to improve the bottom line.

Framework

The procurement process framework, as shown in Figure 1.1, starts with a mission and vision, and consists of two parallel processes: managing the procurement process and executing the purchasing transactions. Managing the procurement process includes sourcing (the focus of this book), partnering, performance metrics, and knowledge management. Executing the purchasing transactions consists of determining requirements, ordering, receiving, storing, issuing, and paying. This framework provides the context for supplier selection.

Mission and Vision

The mission and vision should drive the procurement processes. A lot is said about missions and visions, but what are they? Mission is defining what type of business and organization you are in, i.e., the present. Vision is defining what kind of business and organization you wish to become, i.e., the future. While the mission may be somewhat matter of fact, the vision should have elements of inspiration. Each results in objectives.

Consider Intel's objective to "double machine per-

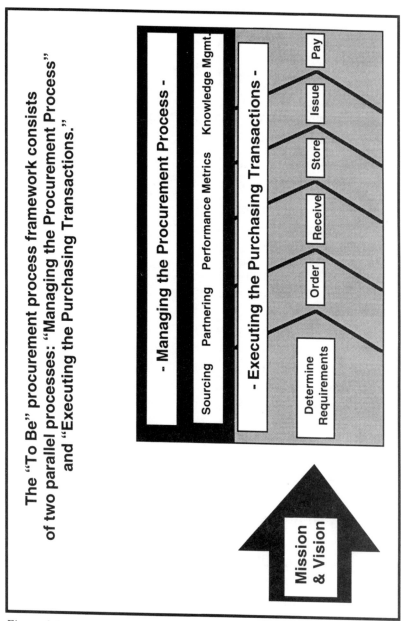

The "To Be" procurement process framework consists of two parallel processes: "Managing the Procurement Process" and "Executing the Purchasing Transactions."

- Managing the Procurement Process -

Sourcing   Partnering   Performance Metrics   Knowledge Mgmt.

- Executing the Purchasing Transactions -

Determine Requirements   Order   Receive   Store   Issue   Pay

Mission & Vision

Figure 1.1

formance at every price point every year." Five potential procurement implications from this goal may include:

- reduce size of purchased components without compromising performance or quality.

- increase processing speed of critical components without increasing cost.

- align component suppliers to develop "combination" solutions (e.g. combine 5 parts into 1).

- stabilize prices, i.e., offset inflation and other increases through continuous improvements and new design solutions.

- tie performance improvements to both purchasing contracts and future sourcing decisions.

In terms of developing the procurement mission and vision, they should align with your overall company's mission and vision. And, the leading executive should involve members of his/her team and others in the organization in defining and confirming both.

The information you need is:

My company's mission is: _____

_____

My company's vision is: _____

_____

Procurement's mission is: _____

_____

Procurement's vision is: _____

_____

Now, think about changes you would make to procurement's mission and vision based on your company's mission and vision, and the procurement processes the mission and vision need to drive. Are they clear? Could you share them in an elevator ride? Could you explain them to a stranger? Is the vision inspirational? Do people in your organization know it and understand it? Is it a focal point? Is it a rallying cry? These are all questions to ask yourself and discuss with your associates. It is critical you know your mission and vision as you embark on improving your supplier selection.

Using the Intel example above, identify five procurement implications of your company's vision:

_____

_____

_____

_____

_____

Strategic Sourcing Imperative

In Chapter Two, we address the strategic sourcing imperative. This includes driving forces and implications, the operations connection, costs for a typical manufacturing company, key success factors, and the benefits and impacts on net income of strategic sourcing. Consider that operations usually contains 60-70% of assets employed, personnel, margin performance, and costs of goods sold (COGS). And, for a typical manufacturing company, 55% of COGS are purchased materials. A 1%

reduction in COGS delivers the same margin lift as 12-18% sales growth. We share an example where one food company reduced material cost by 2% and increased net income by 17%.

Situation Analysis

In Chapter Three, we address situation analysis. This includes key procurement processes, differentiating between tactical buying and strategic sourcing, identifying types of purchases, and how to establish a baseline. Buying versus sourcing comparisons are made against seven elements: price, quality, service, technology, partnership, globalization/localization, and market trends. In addition, a criticality of supply "risk" versus complexity of supply "cost" matrix is shared where you can categorize your purchases into one of four quadrants: noncritical, high dependency, strategic high value, and financial importance.

Supply Strategy

In Chapter Four, we address supply strategy. This includes identifying key market criteria, gathering internal and external data, sole- versus single- versus multi-sourcing, strategic sourcing plans, and some best practice strategies. Examples of key market criteria are: high volume purchased in market, high value purchased in market, limited production capacity in total worldwide demand or inability to meet peaks/valleys, government regulated, criticality to manufacturing process, long lead times, and specialized technology. In addition, some information on current and emerging best practice strategies is shared, including things like the pantry concept, fact-based negotiations, consortium buying, and facilitating strategic supplier relationships.

Strategic Sourcing

In Chapter Five, we address the heart of supplier selection, strategic sourcing. This includes selection criteria or a global value equation, identifying potential suppliers, cross-functional sourcing teams, and rationalizing suppliers. A long list of potential selection criteria is shared, as well as an example global value equation focused on: price, quality, service, technology, partnership, and globalization/localization. A value indexing methodology, which is an emerging best practice to develop, manage, and execute with cross-functional sourcing teams is shared. How to determine value indexing factors, establish guidelines and weights, and develop an operating system are covered, including an example from an electronics company.

Tactical Buying and Electronic Commerce

In Chapter Six, we address tactical buying and electronic commerce. This includes differences versus sourcing and identifying what is "new" about tactical buying that needs to be considered in supplier selection, the why and how to consolidate volume, centralized versus decentralized procurement, blanket orders, procurement cards, Electronic Data Interchange (EDI), intranets, and the Internet. In light of consolidating volume and reducing the supply base, the benefits of centralized, decentralized, and combination organizations from a procurement standpoint are reviewed. And "work-arounds" or alternatives when an organization is decentralized are provided.

Implementation & Results

In Chapter Seven, we address implementation and results. This includes how to take a balanced approach, have a waved implementation, incorporate change management, and measure performance. Andersen Consulting's change management framework which consists of four components is reviewed. These components include: navigation (for example, understand stakeholders' expectations), leadership (for example, have the procurement initiative be one of the top three to five priorities), ownership (for example, formally identifying and developing change agents), and enablement (for example, training and performance management). In terms of measuring performance, industry-standard examples of procurement measures are provided, the evils of purchase price variance (PPV) discussed, and benchmarks for the electronics and consumer products industries shared. The need to track, analyze, and report results and tie them to evaluations and incentives is also addressed.

Summary

When you finish this book you should be able to continuously improve how you do supplier selection for your company.

STRATEGIC
SOURCING
IMPERATIVE

CHAPTER TWO

Introduction

In this chapter we address the strategic sourcing imperative. This includes driving forces and implications, the operations connection, costs for a typical manufacturing company, key success factors, and the benefits and impacts on net income of strategic sourcing. Consider that operations usually contains 60-70% of assets employed, personnel, margin performance, and costs of goods sold (COGS). And, for a typical manufacturing company, 55% of COGS are purchased materials. A 1% reduction in COGS delivers the same margin lift as 12-18% sales growth. We share an example where one food company reduced material cost by 2% and increased net income by 17%.

Driving Forces/Implications

Strategic sourcing is a process of acquiring goods and services and developing and managing supplier relationships in a way that helps achieve the imperatives of a business. Imperatives of a business are driven by both macro and micro market imperatives.

Macro market imperatives include sophistication of customer and consumer demands, higher customer and consumer expectations, fundamental shifts in the industry infrastructure, and shareholder expectations. We will address each of these in turn.

Sophistication of customer and consumer demands includes things like variety, convenience, one-stop service, freshness, quality, healthfulness, and environmentally conscious. Sophistication like this drives new businesses like Wild Oats, a "natural" supermarket chain. It also drives changes in what products and services are offered, and how they are offered. This obviously impacts how goods and services need to be procured.

For example, if your company wants to change its products and distribution in order to respond to the "freshness" demand or make "fresh" your value proposition, this may impact the types of ingredients you buy, the lead time you need, and so forth. Think about Anheuser-Busch, Inc.'s "born on date" addition to its product and its Bud campaign centered around freshness (e.g. "step away from the funky beer"). Identify three implications you think this may have on the sourcing process:

1. _____

2. _____

3. _____

Not surprisingly, this sophistication of demands also corresponds with higher customer and consumer expectations in three areas: value, speed, and service.

Fundamental shifts in the industry infrastructure include the emergence and growth of alternative channels. For example, hypermarkets or "category killers" (e.g. Toys R Us), wholesale clubs (e.g. Sam's Club), supercenters (WalMart), deep discounters, home shopping (e.g. mail order), and electronic commerce (e.g. Internet). This changes the competitive landscape, distribution channels, what and how products and services are marketed, and in turn how goods and services are sourced. If your company were to enter the wholesale club channel with an existing product, identify five procurement implications:

Channel: Wholesale Club
Product:

Procurement Implications:

1. _____

2. _____

3. _____

4. _____

5. _____

Under, over, and around these macro market imperatives are shareholder expectations. These may be public or private shareholder expectations depending on your type of company, but there are always expectations. These expectations often take the form of Return on Investment (ROI), Return on Net Assets (RONA), Return on Capital Employed (ROCE), and Earnings Before Interest and Taxes (EBIT). However, for many manufacturers, these expectations are increasingly taking the form of Economic Value Added (EVA).

Economic value is "the value of an earning asset in an efficient market." EVA is a way to determine whether a business is increasing shareholder value, and equals after-tax operating profit minus the cost of capital. Looking at an example for a national convenience store company:

After-Tax Profits
$ 26.2MM Operating Profit (Earnings Before
Interest and Taxes)
- 10.1MM Taxes (@ 38.5%)

$ 16.1MM

Cost of Capital
10.0% Weighted Average Cost (62% Debt @ 5.0%
38% Equity @ 18.2%)
x $ 240.8MM Total Capital

$ 24.1MM
EVA
($ 8.0MM)

In spite of historically high profits at this company, the shareholders (or capital providers) were dissatisfied, in this case because of a negative $8.0MM EVA. This firm was ripe for a takeover, and in fact has merged with a competitor.

The implications of EVA for procurement and sourcing lie in what can be done to improve EVA, things which include: increasing sales, reducing COGS, reducing capital, investing capital in projects with positive EVA, and reducing expenses.

Micro market imperatives include pricing, customer service, quality, market share, speed to market, growth, profitability, globalization, technology, and the executive agenda. We'll address the executive agenda here.

The emerging executive agenda is tied to the macro and micro market imperatives and includes: fueling the organization's growth engine; reshaping the business to the emerging marketplace; investing in technology for impact; achieving a competitive level of operations excellence; fostering a high performing work force, organization, and culture; and determining the global direction. And, as we saw in Chapter One, the executive drives the company's overall mission and vision, which in turn scopes procurement's mission and vision.

These macro and micro market imperatives, increasing competitiveness, and potential benefit (which we will address more in the remainder of this chapter), are just some of the strategic sourcing drivers. A list of the strategic sourcing drivers includes:

- Purchases represent over 50% of COGS
- Companies have limited partnership arrangements with current supply base
- Agreements do not minimize total cost
- Minimal focus on noninventory purchases
- High exposure of market volatility
- Proliferation of suppliers
- Purchasing organization misaligned
- Need for cost reduction
- Globalization of supply chain

The strategic sourcing implications include:
- Critical to overall competitiveness
- Highly leveraged benefits
- Short- and long-term impact to the bottom line
- High payback (3 to 6 months in some cases)
- Requires different thinking and focused attention
- Challenges existing processes, practices, and supply base
- Different performance measures
- Alternative incentives (e.g. recognition, rewards, compensation, and bonuses)
- Requires highly specialized knowledge in some areas (e.g. legal and tariff issues with suppliers with global delivery capability)

Operations Connection

Consider that operations usually contains 60-70% of assets employed, personnel, margin performance, and

COGS. In this context, operations is defined as the structure used to deliver products and services from "source to shelf," and the process capabilities in supply, manufacturing, and flow management required to fulfill demand. Procurement is part of the fulfill demand process.

Historically, misaligned and conflicting operating goals within operations have inhibited overall system performance by being focused on functional goals that are internally driven versus customer or consumer driven. Examples of functional goals are shown in the functional silos in Figure 2.1.

As shown in Figure 2.1, most procurement professionals target price. However, there are numerous leverage points to enhance the negotiation of the final transaction price, including: volume leverage, hedging, performance and incentive structures, gain sharing, eliminating rebates, supplier's cost structure, and guaranteed reductions.

The ways in which materials are used or consumed represents one of the largest potential sources for reduction in total cost of ownership. Examples, which clearly cut across functional silos, include: end product cost, standardization, elimination, functional equivalents, mix shifting, extended life products, scrap, transportation, recycling, product design, product specifications, and customer and product variations.

Waste must also be removed from all aspects of the supply chain, again cutting across functional silos and focusing on administrative activities and business pro-

Procurement	Manufacturing	Distribution	Sales & Customer Service
Low purchase price	Few line change-overs	Low inventories	High inventories
Stable require-ments	Stable schedule	Long lead times	High service levels
Long lead times	Long run length	Fast replenishment to Distribution Centers (DCs)	Regional stocking and availability
Multiple suppliers	Limited geography	Lowest-cost transportation	Customized value-added services
Few partnerships	Limited relation-ships with contractors	Minimal value-added capabili-ties	"Push" demand philosophy (e.g. promotions)
		Fixed capacity and capabilities	Volume versus profit mentality

Figure 2.1

cesses. Examples of areas to look at include: obsolete inventory, payables, store/ready to use inventory, purchase order processing, environmental and safety, consolidated invoicing, Just-In-Time (JIT) deliveries, stockless inventory, electronic ordering and invoicing, procurement cards, occupancy costs, quality, material planning, receiving, Internet technology, and performance reporting. Which of these areas are the most promising in your company? Can you think of any other areas?

1. _____

2. _____

3. _____

4. _____

5. _____

Breaking out of the traditional, functional silo mode is critical to achieve the overall company's mission and vision. Optimizing the parts usually does not result in optimizing the whole. So what does this mean to procurement and sourcing? It means procurement and sourcing needs to be looked at in the larger context of operations and the company, versus in functional isolation.

Looking at a different type of example, consider DuPont and their stated goal of doubling shareholder value by 2002. DuPont operates in a variety of businesses, including chemicals, textiles, plastics, and oil, and produces a variety of products, including Kevlar and Teflon. Supporting these businesses and their multiple

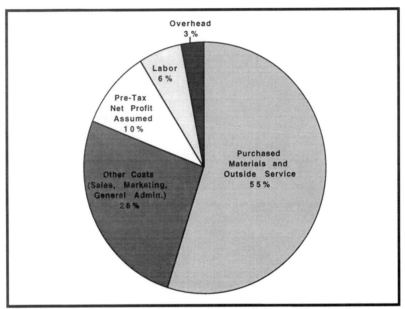

Figure 2.2

operations from an information systems standpoint would be a challenge. If you were the procurement liaison with the Chief Information Officer (CIO) who wanted to reduce information systems costs to DuPont, what kinds of things would you do?

1. _____

2. _____

3. _____

In the early 1990s, DuPont's CIO set out to reduce costs. Over the course of five years, the annualized costs were reduced from $1.2B to $690MM, giving DuPont the lowest IT costs as a percentage of sales in the industry. At the same time, some technological innovations were pursued and introduced with DuPont (e.g. World Wide Web intranets). After accomplishing what they could internally, they asked the question: "What's the next dimension?" For them, the answer was a 10-year strategic outsourcing arrangement. In addition to reducing costs by a least an additional 5%, DuPont considers this arrangement more dynamic and flexible, i.e., leading-edge solutions are provided by expert IT providers, and DuPont will have "on demand" IT support which can be added or subtracted when businesses are sold or acquired.

Costs For A Typical Manufacturing Company

Purchased materials and outside services often make up 55% of manufacturing company revenue. Consider the decomposition of revenue as shown in Figure 2.2 from "Purchasing's New Muscle," *Fortune*, February 20, 1995.

What percent of purchased materials and outside services make up revenue in your company? Using the previous example, decompose your company's revenue:

	$MM	%
Purchased Materials & Outside Services	_____	_____
Overhead	_____	_____
Labor	_____	_____
Pre-Tax Net Profit	_____	_____
Other Costs (SG&A)	_____	_____
Totals	_____	100%

Key Success Factors

There are seven key success factors which drive and measure performance across functional silos within operations:

Innovation - driving out competitive advantage through strategic relationships across the value chain and by building a true learning organization

Precision - synchronization of information and product flows with a high degree of exactness to customer or consumer demand (e.g. make to actual demand versus forecast)

Responsiveness/Flexibility - frequent production and distribution of every Stock Keeping Unit (SKU) while maintaining or increasing capacity

Reliability - predictable, repeatable, consistent supplier and operational performance

Quality - meeting customer- or consumer-centered specifications, driven by appropriate level of ownership and measurements, including safety and environmental goals

Asset Utilization - effective utilization of buildings, space, equipment, and human assets to maximize return on invested capital

Cost to Serve - meet or exceed conversion (labor, materials, etc.) and inventory (working capital, storage, etc.) cost targets to deliver products to customers or consumers

Benefits/Impact On Net Income

These seven key success factors can have a profound

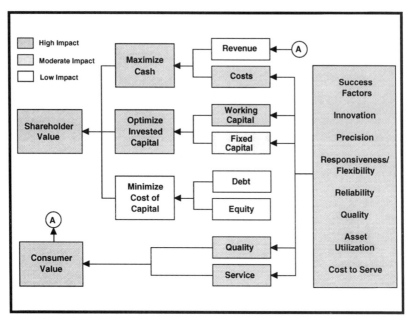

Figure 2.3

impact on shareholder and consumer value. Areas with high, moderate, and low impact are noted by the shading in Figure 2.3.

As quoted in *Fortune*, February 20, 1995, "When the goal is boosting profits by dramatically lowering costs, a business should look first to what it buys." The cost competitiveness and overall market position can often depend upon the effectiveness of strategically managing the procurement area, of which sourcing is a critical component.

In terms of the potential impact on net income, with material costs representing 55% of revenue, a 5% decrease in material costs can increase net income by 27% for a $1B company. The range of potential in this example is shown in Figure 2.4.

	Baseline	% Improvement		
		5%	10%	15%
Revenue	$1,000	1,000	1,000	1,000
		% Improvement		
	Baseline	5%	10%	15%
COGS				
* Material	550	523	495	468
* Labor/Overhead	225	225	225	225
Gross Margin	225	252	280	307
Operating Expenses	125	125	125	125
Net Income (Before Taxes)	100	127	155	182
% Increase		27%	55%	82%

Figure 2.4

Using the example in Figure 2.4, determine the impact on net income you would have in your company for similar 5%, 10%, and 15% improvements in material costs.

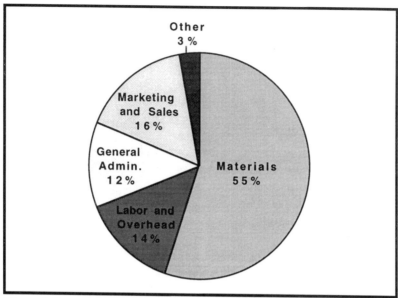

Figure 2.5

($MM)

	Baseline	% Improvement		
		5%	10%	15%
Revenue	———	——	——	——

	Baseline	% Improvement		
		5%	10%	15%
COGS				
* Material	——	——	——	——
* Labor/Overhead	——	——	——	——
Gross Margin	——	——	——	——
Operating Expenses	——	——	——	——
Net Income (Before Taxes)	——	——	——	——
% Increase		——	——	——

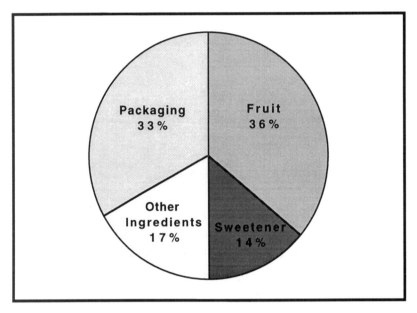

Figure 2.6

Now, let's consider a food company example. This company is fairly representative of other manufacturers in that its materials costs are 55%, as shown in Figure 2.5. A further breakdown of material costs is shown in Figure 2.6.

Using materials costs at 52% of revenue (55% of COGS), a 2% decrease in material cost can increase net income by 17%, as shown in Figure 2.7.

Strategic sourcing can also be utilized to reverse the trend of absorbing inflation. The typical manufacturer absorbs 3% inflation in total procurement system costs per year. This trend can be reversed with a philosophy of declining and stabilizing costs. For example, the most successful consumer products companies have been able

($MM)	Baseline	After
Revenue	$600	600
COGS		
* Material	312	306
* Labor/Overhead	78	78
Gross Margin	210	216
Operating Expenses	174	174
Net Income (Before Taxes)	36	42
% Increase		17%

Figure 2.7

to stabilize the costs of materials and services over the past 10-15 years. In addition to financial benefits, significant operational improvements are driven by strategic sourcing, including:

- improved quality.
- reduced cycle time.
- increased flexibility and responsiveness.
- improved supplier delivery performance.
- increased fill rates.
- improved productivity.
- improved capability (e.g. personnel).
- improved customer satisfaction.

While actual results will vary, some specific commodity results you can use for cost reduction benchmarks are shown in Figure 2.8.

Retail Industry		MRO & Services		Direct Material	
Commodity	%	Commodity	%	Commodity	%
Car batteries	25	Oil and lubricants	42	Lab supplies	47
Auto tires	17	Elec. supplies	31	Medical supplies	37
Wallpaper	12	Bearings	26	Flexible pkg	33
Auto parts	7	PC hdwe/sfwe/support	25	Gases	33
Furniture	6	Business forms	22	Punches and dies	30
Major appliances	5	Copiers	22	Folding ctns	25
Electronics	4	Office supplies	21	Elec. products	22
		Safety supplies	20	Plastic products	22
		Solid waste disposal	20	Corrugated cntnrs	19
		Freight	19	Thermoformed parts	18
		Hazardous waste disp	18	Motors	17
		Rental cars	13	Automotive parts	16
		Contract labor	13	Molded plastic bottles	15
		Travel	10	Power equip prods	15
		Electricity	8	Resins	12
		Guard/security services	8	Brick	12
				Glass	12
				Oil and lubricants	11
				Chemicals	10
				Dextrose	9
				Coal	9
				Bicycle parts	8
				Adhesives	7
				Resins	7

Figure 2.8

Summary

In this chapter we addressed the strategic sourcing imperative. This included driving forces and implications, the operations connection, costs for a typical manufacturing company, key success factors, and the benefits and impacts on net income of strategic sourcing. In several examples we showed a "baseline." In Chapter Three we address situation analysis, which includes establishing baselines.

SITUATION ANALYSIS

CHAPTER THREE

Introduction

In this chapter we address situation analysis. This includes key procurement processes, differentiating between tactical buying and strategic sourcing, identifying types of purchases, and how to establish a baseline. Buying versus sourcing comparisons are made against seven elements: price, quality, service, technology, partnership, globalization/localization, and market trends. In addition, a criticality of supply "risk" versus complexity of supply "cost" matrix is shared where you can categorize your purchases into one of four quadrants: noncritical, high dependency, strategic high value, and financial importance.

Key Processes

As shown in Chapter One, Figure 1.1, the procurement process framework consists of two parallel processes that are both part of the fulfill demand process addressed in Chapter Two: managing the procurement process and executing the purchasing transactions. Managing the procurement process includes sourcing (the focus of this book), partnering, performance metrics, and knowledge management. Executing the purchasing transactions consists of determining requirements, ordering, receiving, storing, issuing, and paying.

As part of business process design process, especially when combined with a global technology solution, these processes are often grouped into subprocesses. For example, in designing the "To Be" procurement processes for an electronics firm, five key subprocesses were identified: 1) demand planning, 2) sourcing, 3) order processing, 4) inventory and materials management, and 5) invoice verification and payment. We will address each of these in turn, but go into more detail on the sourcing subprocess example.

For the electronics firm, demand planning consisted of four activities: 1) spare parts planning, 2) raw materials purchase planning, 3) equipment investment planning, and 4) purchase plan consolidation.

The sourcing subprocess is primarily strategic in nature. For the electronics firm, sourcing consisted of seven activities: 1) supplier knowledge management, 2) supplier strategy development, 3) investment analysis, 4) supplier

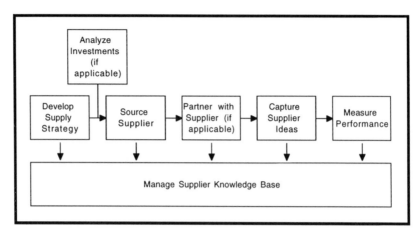

Figure 3.1

sourcing, 5) supplier partnering, 6) supplier idea capturing, and 7) performance measuring. How these activities related to one another is shown in Figure 3.1.

The objective of each of these activities and some of their subactivities are:

Supplier Knowledge Management – The objective of this activity is to build and maintain a repository of critical supply information, including historical performance. Some subactivities include determining the information you want to capture in the supplier knowledge base, defining the data fields and developing the tables and formulas in an integrated information system, gathering and maintaining information real time, and providing on-line global accessibility.

Supplier Strategy Development - The objective of this activity is to determine key markets, and then develop supply strategies for the key markets. Some subactivities include reviewing key market identification criteria, gathering external data (trends, competition, cost structure, technology changes, potential suppliers, etc.), gathering internal data (requirements, relative importance of value equation elements, suppliers' historical performance, cross-functional input, etc.), analyzing the data and assessing risks, and modifying or developing new strategies.

Investment Analysis – The objective of this activity is to evaluate the financial and strategic impacts of proposed investments. This activity is primarily equipment focused, but can also be related to joint technology and/or localization investments. Some subactivities include determining investment criteria, determining if external (e.g. government) funding is available, preparing investment proposals, performing financial and strategic analyses on proposals, and seeking management approval.

Supplier Sourcing – The objective of this activity is to determine the source for raw materials, equipment, and spare parts which are strategic (versus tactical) in nature. Some subactivities include reviewing key market supply strategies, determining relative importance of global value equation criteria, accessing the supplier knowledge base, identifying potential suppliers, assessing suppliers' capabilities, evaluating the absolute and relative suppliers' abilities to meet requirements, selecting suppliers utilizing global value equation criteria, updating the knowledge base and the supply strategy, and communicating the decision internally and externally.

Supplier Partnering – The objective of this activity is to screen current and potential suppliers for their strategic importance, determine a business case for a partnership, and develop and manage the partnership while measuring the benefits over time. Some subactivities include establishing listening posts to receive referrals, determining if the supplier is a potential strategic supplier of the future, identifying if the supplier is in a key market, preparing a business case for partnership, determining if a partnership should be pursued, developing a straw model detailed design of the partnership, meeting with the supplier to review and refine the design and agree on mutual benefits and performance measures, developing and managing the partnership, and tracking and measuring performance and mutual benefits.

Supplier Idea Capturing – The objective of this activity is to provide a formal channel for capturing and incorporating suppliers' ideas into current and future processes and products. Some subactivities include classifying suppliers by Tier 1 (suppliers in key markets or partnerships), Tier 2 (suppliers not in Tier 1 or Tier 3), and Tier 3 (potential suppliers), meeting with Tier 1 suppliers quarterly to request ideas, capturing Tier 2 suppliers' ideas as they occur, meeting with Tier 3 suppliers to solicit ideas and basis for business, evaluating ideas and identifying early (quick) wins, prioritizing ideas, developing action plans for the "Top 10" ideas, and implementing the action plans.

Performance Measuring – The objective of this activity is to measure, track, and report performance on two fronts: internal procurement process performance, and external suppliers' performance; and in both cases, take corrective action where warranted. Some subactivities include identifying key performance measures, collecting and consolidating data, analyzing data and determining trends, summarize what's working and not working, conducting root cause analyses on what's not working, developing improvement plans, and implementing improvement plans. In the case of suppliers, performance measuring needs to be integral to formal supplier evaluation programs and/or certification programs.

The process flows for each of these activities is beyond the scope of this book. However, for perspective, the "To Be" sourcing subprocess designed for the electronics firm represented differences in five key areas: simpler processes, organization design, performance measures, change management, and differentiated risk/complexity strategies. The "As Is" versus "To Be" differences are shown in Figure 3.2.

Finishing addressing the five key subprocesses identified for the electronics firm, the third subprocess, order processing, consisted of four activities: 1) requisitioning, 2) request for quotation (RFQ), 3) negotiating and contracting, and 4) purchasing order processing.

Inventory and materials management consisted of eight activities: 1) inventory management, 2) releasing, 3) inbound shipping, 4) customs clearance, 5) central

"As Is"	➡	"To Be"
• Transaction and approval intense; time consuming	Simpler Processes	• Simpler, more flexible, less time consuming processes
• Fractured; duplicate responsibilities; purchases not always leveraged; low spans of control	Organization Design	• Reorganized to leverage buying power, and separate strategic and tactical buying
• Only 12% average of suppliers formally evaluated; internal measures cost focused; no alignment across functions; little tracking; no tie to reward system	Performance Measures	• Formal, objective, balanced and customer focused performance measures internally and with suppliers; tied to reward system
• Poor communication; no sense of community across functions; low morale; no singular focus for the future	Change Management	• Singular mission/vision focus; formal and routine communication; increased morale
• Key market criteria, and strategic vs. tactical criteria does not formally exist; there aren't different strategies for different risk/complexity combinations	Differentiated Risk/ Complexity Strategies	• Key market criteria defined; strategic vs. tactical criteria defined; differentiated strategies for different risk/complexity combinations

Figure 3.2

receiving, 6) incoming quality control, 7) warehouse management, and 8) dispatch to end users.

Invoice verification and payment consisted of two areas: 1) processing invoices and three-way matching, and 2) claims.

Next we turn our attention to the difference between tactical buying and strategic sourcing.

Tactical Buying Versus Strategic Sourcing

In general, tactical buying is focused on transactions and nonstrategic material buying. As such, it is closely aligned with the "ordering" portion of the executing the purchasing transactions process. Strategic sourcing, on the other hand, is focused on acquiring goods and services and developing and managing supplier relationships in a way that helps achieve the imperatives of a business. As such, it is closely aligned with the "sourcing" portion of managing the procurement process.

While this seems pretty straightforward, there is a tendency in most firms to classify most materials as strategic and organize people and work accordingly. As a result, the truly strategic materials suffer from lack of focus and attention, and resources are wasted on "over buying" tactical materials. In order to overcome this tendency, criteria needs to be established to classify a material as something that should be tactically bought or strategically sourced. For example, criteria developed for an electronics firm included price, quality, service, technology, partnership, globalization/localization, and market trends. As you will see in Chapter Five, this criteria is often closely related to selection criteria and the global value equation.

Using this criteria as an example, list criteria you currently use, or could use, to classify a material as something that should be tactically bought or strategically sourced.

1. _____
2. _____
3. _____
4. _____
5. _____
6. _____
7. _____

Buying (Tactical)	Criteria	Sourcing (Strategic)
• Stable, fluctuations limited, local currency	Price	• Unbounded increases/decreases, foreign currency
• ISO 9000 certified, good quality audit results, good quality history	Quality	• New specifications, new suppliers, poor quality history
• Availability non-critical to production, good on-time delivery performance, EDI, blanket orders, Vendor Managed Inventory (VMI)	Service	• Availability critical to production, poor on-time delivery performance, inventory level control, long lead times, new VMI arrangements
• No variations to specifications desired	Technology	• Specification variations desired, exclusivity arrangements, patents, joint (technology) developments
• Stable supplier/supply, long-term relationship	Partnership	• Unstable supplier/supply, limited suppliers, new relationships, competitors as suppliers, potential mergers and acquisitions (M&A)
• Close to using facility	Globalization/ Localization	• Monopoly risk, third party funding, joint (localization) developments
• Stable, flat, predictable	Market Trends	• Volatile, unpredictable, competitors trends within market

Figure 3.3

For the electronics firm, the descriptors that went with this criteria to distinguish between buying (tactical) versus sourcing (strategic) are shown in Figure 3.3.

In Figure 3.3a, using the criteria you listed, and the descriptors example, write descriptors which go along with your criteria to distinguish between buying (tactical) versus sourcing (strategic) at your company.

As shown in Figure 3.3, a number of the descriptors contained words related to risk, including: limited versus unbounded, established versus new, good versus poor, noncritical versus critical, no variation to variations desired, stable versus unstable, and predictable versus volatile. Managing risk and complexity is an important consideration in distinguishing between tactical buying and strategic sourcing.

Buying (Tactical)	*Your Criteria*	*Sourcing (Strategic)*

Figure 3.3a

One way to assess risk and complexity is to utilize a criticality of supply "risk" versus complexity of supply "cost" matrix. As shown in Figure 3.4, this matrix consists of four quadrants: 1) noncritical, 2) high dependency, 3) strategic high value, and 4) financial importance.

Referring to the descriptors in each quadrant, it is fairly easy to see tactical buying and materials management skills would dominate in the noncritical quadrant, and strategic sourcing and procurement skills would dominate in the strategic high value quadrant. While there can be a mixture of tactical buying and strategic sourcing in the high dependency and financial importance quadrants, strategic sourcing is usually more prevalent due to the potential positive and negative impacts.

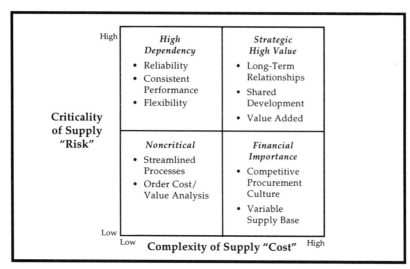

Figure 3.4

A variation of this matrix was utilized for a food company. For example, the relative power of suppliers (external) versus exposure (internal) was examined, and is shown in Figure 3.5.

Another variation of this is the Material Positioning Matrix from the *Supply Management Toolbox* (PT Publications; West Palm Beach, FL). For any commodity you source, the Material Positioning Matrix allows you to rate the degree of influence the commodity has on your competitiveness, as well the procurement risk you face when sourcing.

Types Of Purchases

The types of goods and services purchased which need to be examined for tactical buying or strategic sourcing generally include six types: 1) ingredients/raw

	High		
		I Materials which support the business but are difficult to source	*II* Materials which are critical to the business and difficult to source
Relative Power of Suppliers (External)		*III* Materials which support the business and are relatively easy to source	*IV* Materials which are critical to the business but may be relatively easy to source
	Low		
		Low **Exposure (Internal)** High	

Figure 3.5

materials; 2) packaging materials; 3) Maintenance, Repair, & Operating (MRO) supplies; 4) equipment and capital; 5) contractors and services; and 6) utilities. The

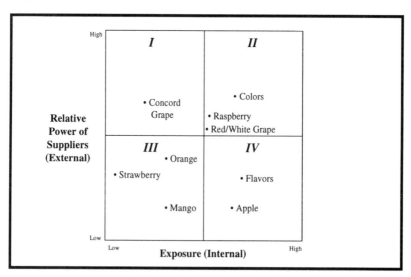

Figure 3.6

first two types, ingredients/raw materials and packaging materials, are considered "direct," i.e., they go directly into the final goods and services. The remaining four types are considered "indirect," i.e., they support the production of final goods and services.

Utilizing the example food company matrix, Figure 3.6 shows how some of their ingredients/raw materials were plotted.

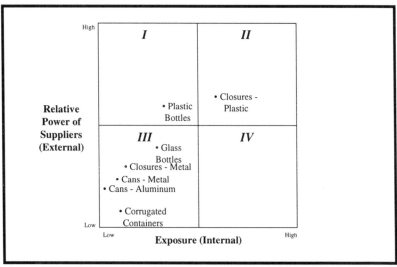

Figure 3.7

Utilizing the same example food company matrix, Figure 3.7 shows how some of their packaging materials were plotted.

Using the food company matrix and examples above, select either ingredients/raw materials or packaging materials, and plot some materials for your company in Figure 3.7a.

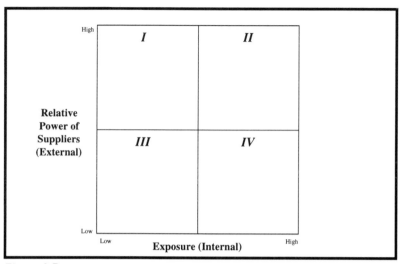

Figure 3.7a

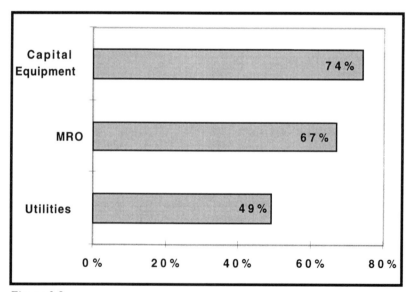

Figure 3.8

Relative to MRO, equipment and capital, and utilities, the percent of spending in these categories controlled by Procurement in manufacturing organizations as reported in a 1995 CAPS Purchasing of Nontraditional Goods and Services study is shown in Figure 3.8.

Contractors and services tends to be a mixed bag, including high-end services like management consultants, technology outsourcing, etc. and low-end services like uniforms, lawn cutting, etc.

Baseline

It is important to establish a "baseline" of the "As Is" situation in order to develop the "To Be" and identify gaps and opportunities. A baseline can be thought of as a profile. A profile of purchases should include purchases by type, by to and from locations, leveraging, organization, and internal and external views of procurement. We will address each of these in turn.

A profile of purchases by type involves determining the amount of currency spent on each of the types of purchases: 1) ingredients/raw materials, 2) packaging materials, 3) MRO supplies, 4) equipment and capital, 5) contractors and services, and 6) utilities. An example for a food company, which includes five of these six types, is shown in Figure 3.9.

Breaking the largest area, packaging, down further, the packaging profile for the food company is shown in Figure 3.10.

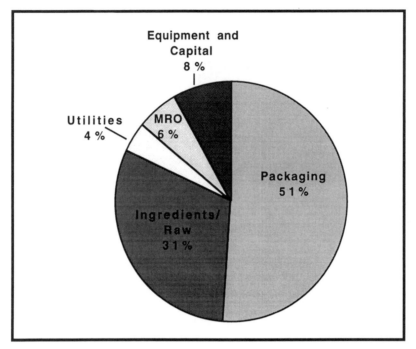

Figure 3.9

Using the six types of purchases, and the food company example, profile the purchases for your company
by type.

	Annual Expenditures (MM)	Annual Expenditures (%)
Ingredients/Raw Materials	$ _____	_____ %
Packaging Materials	$ _____	_____ %
MRO Supplies	$ _____	_____ %
Equipment & Capital	$ _____	_____ %

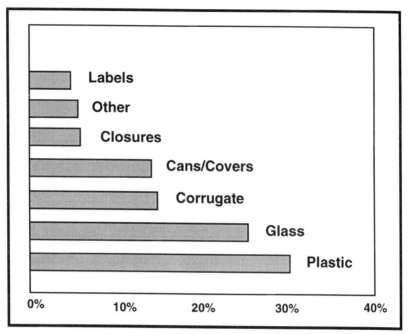

Figure 3.10

Contractors & Services	$ _____	_____ %
Utilities	$ _____	_____ %
Totals	$ _____	100 %

A profile of purchases by to and from locations includes determining the number of locations served by a particular purchase (e.g. plants), and the locations purchases are from (e.g. countries). An example of each for an electronics company is shown in Figure 3.11 and Figure 3.12.

A profile of purchases by leveraging includes look-ing at the numbers of locations served (Figure 3.11), the percent of suppliers making up 80% of the purchasing expenditures (the 80/20 Rule), and the type and length of contracts. An example of the percentage of suppliers making up 80% of the ingredients/raw materials for an electronics company is shown in Figure 3.13, and an example of the type and length of contracts for the same materials and company is shown in Figure 3.14.

In Figure 3.13, 15% of the suppliers account for 80% of the purchases, which is better than the 80/20 Rule. In Figure 3.14, 63% of the purchases are done on a spot basis, providing a lot of opportunity to leverage both volume and length of relationship (and reduce the number and cost of transactions).

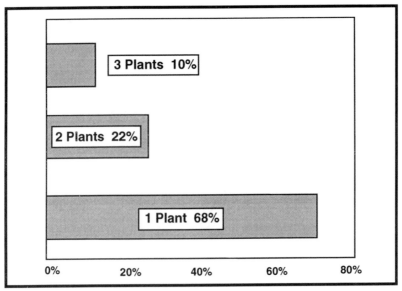

Figure 3.11

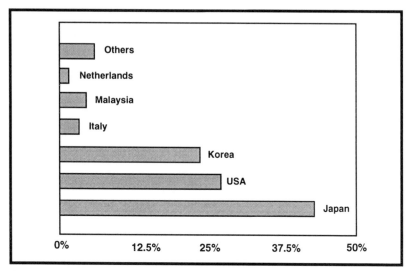

Figure 3.12

A profile of purchases by organization includes determining the number and location of people, reporting relationships, spans of control, and the generalists versus specialists mix. An example of the generalists versus specialists mix for the electronics company is shown in Figure 3.15.

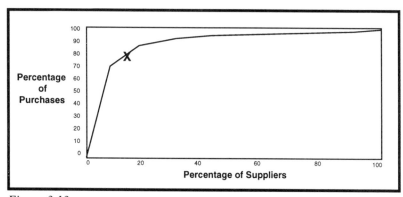

Figure 3.13

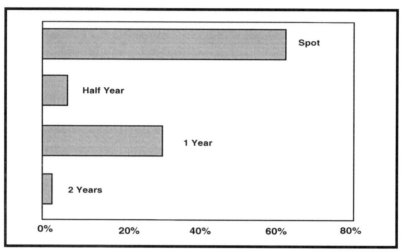

Figure 3.14

As shown in this example, 54% of the procurement personnel are generalists, that is, focusing on more than one type of purchases (e.g. both ingredients/raw materials and packaging materials). For this organization, this percent is too high and represents an opportunity for more focus.

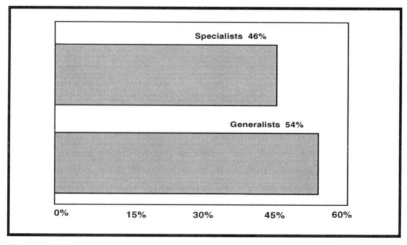

Figure 3.15

Another essential element of establishing a baseline is determining how procurement is viewed both internally and externally. In order to obtain the internal view, it is important to find out from procurement and others what they think about procurement, and why they think that way. In order to obtain the external view, often referred to as the "voice of the supplier," it is important to find out from suppliers what they think about the company and procurement, and why they think that way.

While the methodologies to obtain these points of view are beyond the scope of this book, they include surveys, focus groups, and interviews.

Summary

In this chapter we addressed situation analysis. This included key procurement processes, differentiating between tactical buying and strategic sourcing, identifying types of purchases, and how to establish a baseline. In the procurement processes we introduced the concept of key market criteria. In Chapter Four, we address supply strategy, including key market criteria.

Introduction

In this chapter we address supply strategy. This includes identifying key market criteria, gathering internal and external data, sole- versus single- versus multi-sourcing, strategic sourcing plans, and some best practice strategies.

As we reviewed in Chapter Three, one of the activities included in the sourcing subprocess is supplier strategy development. The objective of this activity is to determine key markets, and then develop supply strategies for the key markets. In order to further set the context for Chapter Four, an example process flow for this activity is shown in Figure 4.1.

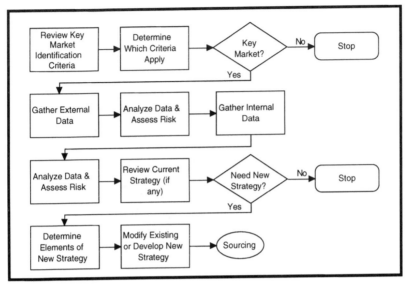

Figure 4.1

Key Market Criteria

As you can see from the process flow, before this activity can begin, key market criteria need to be developed. For example, key market criteria developed for a semiconductor company are:

- High volume purchased in the market
- High value purchased in the market
- Limited production capacity in total worldwide demand or inability to meet peaks and valleys
- Government regulated (e.g. imports) or overall trade pacts (e.g. WTO) in effect
- Critical to manufacturing process (impacts ability to run)
- Long lead times
- Specialized technology

Key market criteria are important to have in order to screen ingredients/raw materials, packaging materials, MRO supplies, equipment, services, and utilities to determine which materials in which key markets warrant supply strategy and partnering priority. Using the example above, list key market criteria for your company.

_____

_____

_____

From the criteria, materials can be screened and their markets identified. Following through on the key market criteria developed for the semiconductor company, a sample of the raw materials, equipment, and spare part "groups" considered "key" is shown in Figure 4.2.

Raw Materials	Equipment	Spare Part "Groups"
• Wafer	• Wafer Inspection	• Vacuum Pump
• Photo Resit	• Steppers	• UV Lamp
• Polyimede	• Etcher	• Quartz Ware
• Mask	• Ion Implanter	• Actuators
• Lead Frame	• Sputter	• Mold Parts

Figure 4.2

In Figure 4.2a, using the key market criteria you identified for your company and the example in Figure 4.2, select three types of purchases (ingredients/raw materials, packaging materials, MRO suppliers, equipment, services, or utilities) and list five specific materials in each type that meet your criteria and should be considered "key."

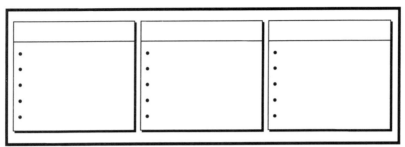

Figure 4.2a

External and Internal Data

As shown in Figure 4.1, gathering and analyzing external and internal data is part of the supplier strategy development activity. We will address gathering external data, gathering internal data, analyzing, and assessing risk in turn.

The type of external data that should be gathered includes information on trends, competition, cost structure, technology changes, potential suppliers, and so forth. Ways to gather this information include environment scanning, surveys, Delphi, focus groups, and interviews. However, environmental scanning and interviews are the most common methods for gathering external data.

Environmental scanning is systematic gathering of information about social, political, economic, and technological developments and about customer and competitor trends in the organization's current and future external world. The technique represents a vigorous initiative to cope with accelerating change and increasing complexity, and establishes a framework for dealing with uncertainty. Environmental scanning systematically and continuously organizes information from a broad range of sources and

considers divergent viewpoints from representative stakeholders and experts. An effective scanning system enables
alerting management to changes in the environment which
are likely to impact the mission, goals, and operations of the
organization. For example, scanners review and write concise summaries of information in related hard and soft
media (periodicals, newspapers, television and radio broad-
casts, Web sites, books, presentations, trade showings, etc.).

When I purchased food ingredient commodities for
the Food Division at Procter & Gamble, some of my respon-
sibilities were to purchase flour, hedge those purchases
with wheat futures, and trade wheat futures with the expec-
tation of making money. Flour met P&G's key market
criteria, and wheat was a key market. If I were doing that job
today, one of things I would do as part of an environment
scan is access ABI/INFORM on the Internet. As an example
of what can be found in subject searches:

- "Wheat" produced 3604 "sites."
- When limited by publication year to 1997,
  "wheat" produced 278 "sites."
- When narrowed by subject, "wheat" and "sup-
  ply" produced 66 "sites."
- When further narrowed by subject, "wheat" and
  "supply" and "price" produced 42 "sites."
- When even further narrowed by subject, "wheat"
  and "supply" and "price" and "imports" pro-
  duced 18 "sites."
- **Among these 18 hits included:**
  - U.S. imports supply behavior: Evidence from
    the 1980s

- State user fees and the dormant Commerce Clause
- Joining the world's trading club
- U.S. international transactions, fourth quarter and year 1996
- Agricultural trends and issues to 2001
- What is the Eleventh Amendment immunity?
- Credit trade finance
- New policy affects commodity risk in agricultural lending
- The world economy
- **What drives agricultural cycles?**
- Ensuring global food security

- **Looking at the abstract for *"What Drives Agricultural Cycles?"* (Jan./Feb. 1997 issue of *Challenge*), several topics or leads for further investigation emerge, including:**
  - Federal Agricultural Improvement and Reform Act (the FAIR Act), April 1996
  - Removal of price supports and production controls
  - Value of the dollar, real interest rates, and exchange rates
  - Europe, Japan, and other producers response in the world market

Of the specific materials you identified as meeting your key market criteria and that should be considered "key," select one to research in ABI/INFORM, and identify four sets of narrowing word concepts you will use in the research.

Specific Material: _____

1st Key Word: _____

2nd Key Word: _____

3rd Key Word: _____

4th Key Word: _____

Interviews should be planned, structured around questions which address emerging issues and developments, and documented with the same rigor as environmental scanning. Interview candidates include suppliers, consultants, industry experts, and academics to name a few. You should plan on making some investment and on confidentiality. Two types of interviews used include: face-to-face and telephone.

Face-to-face interviews should be used when exploring complex questions that require explanatory answers (why, what kind, for whom, etc.). Open-ended questions can be asked. Face-to-face interviews should also be used when asking highly sensitive questions, when all possible responses to a question cannot be anticipated, when respondents are experts in the their field or in upper management, and when time and funds are more plentiful.

Telephone interviews should be used when gathering nonsensitive information with tightly focused questions which can be answered discretely (e.g. yes/no). Forced-choice questions should be asked. Telephone interviews should also be used when gathering strictly numerical information, most or all possible responses are anticipated, and when time and funds are limited.

The type of internal data that should be gathered includes requirements (how much and when), relative importance of value equation elements, suppliers' historical performance, cross-functional input, and so forth. Ways to gather this information include reviewing data and reports, surveys, focus groups, interviews, and direct requests. However, reviewing data and reports, and direct requests, are the most common methods for gathering internal data.

Reviewing existing data and reports can provide the historical perspective. If your company is like many others, data exists, but it has not yet been turned into "intelligence." Different combinations of data and different reports normally need to be requested to be run in order to turn the data into intelligence.

Direct requests are exactly what they sound like: a phone call, e-mail, or memo asking for information or answers to questions that are important to understanding the key market and developing a supply strategy.

After the data is gathered, it needs to be analyzed. The key is to identify and analyze the issues. Analysis puts the pieces of the puzzle together and makes the raw data from all the sources useful for developing a supply strategy and making key sourcing and other decisions. The analysis process should bring out new patterns, linkages, connections, disruptions, and discontinuities, and provide new insights on how changes are likely to affect the key market and supply.

There is no one method of analysis. However, one common method utilized for a situation analysis is SWOT (Strengths, Weaknesses, Opportunities, Threats). Strengths and weaknesses are typically reflective of the internal environment, and opportunities and threats are typically reflective of the external environment. A snapshot of the types of things included is shown in Figure 4.3.

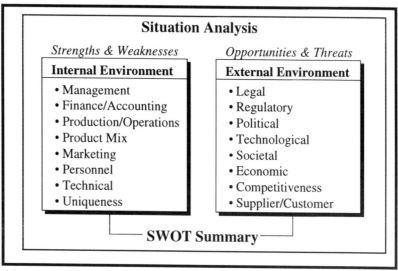

Figure 4.3

As an example of how a SWOT analysis might be applied to a company, review the following analysis for Rollerblade, Inc.'s situation in the early 1990s:

Strengths (S)

- Introduced the category
- Market leader (60%) share
- "Product of the Year" designation
- $350MM market (1993)

- $1B market potential (1998)
- Synergistic ownership relationship (Nordica – #1 ski boot maker)
- Primary market identified (46MM active adults, ages 18-35)
- High promotional activity (high-profile people, cross-promotional tie-ins, videos, demonstration vans, Team Rollerblade)

Weaknesses (W)

- Limited non-tie-in advertising
- Focus on one price segment
- High price end ($100-$400); however, most purchase activity in $139-$199 range
- Sports stores and in-line skating specialty stores
- On a path to try and be all things to all people
- Focus on multiple use segments
- Plans to introduce BladeRunner to low-price end (< $100) and distribute through mass merchandisers
- Plans to open Rollerblade boutiques in some sporting goods stores in U.S.
- Consideration of moving from "pull" to "push" strategy

Opportunities (O)

- Brand name recognition
- Bladegear sportswear extensions and expansions
- Accessory expansions through ownership relationship with Benetton (Prince tennis rackets, Asolo mountain boots, and Kastle skis)

- International expansions
- "Audience" for new product introductions at the New Products Show of the Super Show each Feb. (90K buyers and sellers)

Threats (T)

- Basic in-line skate easy to copy
- 30+ competitors (First Team Sports - 20% share; "Knock-Offs" - 20% share)
- 2K new sports/recreation product introductions per year
- Brand name becoming generic for the activity (e.g. inclusion in dictionary)
- Unknown new technology that could preempt in-line skating

Using the macro SWOT example of Rollerblade, use the same material you selected to research in ABI/IN-FORM and start a micro SWOT analysis of the material you selected based on what you know today.

Specific Material: _____

Strengths (S)

Weaknesses (W)

Opportunities (O)

Threats (T)

A SWOT analysis starts to address the risks, such as competitors, government intervention, and so forth. After the analysis is complete, a specific risk assessment should be completed. The primary types of risks are supply/demand imbalances, supply interruption, technological developments, pricing escalations, disputes, and insufficient skills. Examples for each of the types of risks is shown below.

Supply/Demand Imbalances

- Volume required exceeds volume committed
- Overall market demand grows and customers are put on "allocation"
- Supply throughput/yields do not meet expectations

Supply Interruption

- Natural disasters (weather, etc.)
- Supply disasters (fire, etc.)
- Labor disputes (strikes, sabotage, etc.)
- Captive carrier/transportation blockages (strikes, disasters, etc.)

Technological Developments

- Sole- source cannot produce supplier-developed material
- Non-sourced supplier develops enhanced product, which single-sourced supplier cannot produce (patent, know-how, capital limitations, etc.)

Pricing Escalations

- Price tied to escalator (e.g. Produce Price Index - PPI), but there is no de-escalator
- No competitive market pricing benchmarking/allowances

- Tied to long-term volumes which do not materialize
- No agreement to cost savings/sharing

Disputes

- No or poorly written supply agreement
- No dispute resolution process
- No or limited "if, then" provisions to cover potential scenarios

Insufficient Skills

- Insufficient personnel with required skills in the right positions focused on the right things
- Wrong mix of skills (e.g. purchase order writers versus strategic sourcers)
- Displaced skills (e.g. paper-based versus technology-enabled)
- New skills not being developed (e.g. strategic sourcing, fact-based negotiation, electronic commerce, etc.)

Some of these risks and ways to minimize them are related to sole- versus single- versus multi-sourcing, which we address next. But before we do that, based on what you know today, which of these risks, or additional risks, do you think are present for the same material you selected to research in ABI/INFORM and started a micro SWOT analysis on ?

Specific Material: _____
Risks

Sole- Versus Single- Versus Multi-Sourcing

There are three primary types of sourcing: 1) sole-sourcing, 2) single-sourcing, and 3) multi-sourcing. We will define and address advantages and disadvantages of each, as well as list a number of ways to minimize the risks detailed in the earlier section. Please note the advantages and disadvantages are presented in black and white terms for illustrative purposes; in reality, they are often shades of gray. The definitions and advantages and disadvantages of each type of sourcing are:

Sole-Sourcing – You are in a sole-sourcing situation when there is one and only one source from which to get the goods or services you want to buy. This is usually the case with a unique, patented material (e.g. aspartame). The supplier selection decision here is the same as the material decision, i.e., buy or do without.

Advantages

- You have access to a unique material which supports products demanded in the market place (e.g. diet soft drinks).
- You are aligned with the supplier with the know-how to make leading edge materials.
- It provides the basis for a supplier strategic alliance.
- You focus your resources on one supplier.

Disadvantages

- Balance of power is skewed towards the supplier.
- Unique, patented materials are often priced at a premium.

- You may have a duel labeling requirement in order to get a price reduction (e.g. NutraSweet logo).

- In cases of supply interruption, there is no place else to go.

- Unless jointly developed, material will also be available to your competitors.

- You may get into a long-term requirements contract which: a) you cannot meet, b) you cannot get more than your "allocated" amount, or c) is displaced in the market place by another unique, patented material developed by a different supplier.

Single-Sourcing – You are in a single-sourcing situation when there is more than one source for the goods or services you want to buy, but you chose to only source from one supplier. The supplier selection decision here is which one of the alternatives do you want.

Advantages

- Supplier knows you had a choice, and this brings balance of power to the relationship

- You can use fact of alternatives to bear in selecting a supplier and negotiating terms and conditions.

- It provides the basis for a supplier strategic alliance.

- You focus your resources on one supplier.

Disadvantages

- In cases of supply interruption, it takes time to go someplace else .

- Combined with cases of market place allocations, there may be no place else to go (e.g. during UPS strike, FedEx stopped taking new customers).

Multi-Sourcing – You are in a multi-sourcing situation when there is more than one source for the goods or services you want to buy, and you chose to source from two or more suppliers. The supplier selection decision here is how many sources do you want, and which ones.

Advantages
- Balance of power is skewed towards the purchaser; for tactical buying and transaction-focused purchases, this is an advantage.
- In cases of supply interruption, you have alternatives available quickly.

Disadvantages
- Balance of power is skewed towards the purchaser; for strategic sourcing and value-focused purchases, this is a disadvantage; you are viewed as the enemy
- Fractured volume; lose advantages of leveraging volume
- You have no basis for a supplier strategic alliance.
- Your resources are fractured across multiple suppliers.

These three types of sourcing are illustrated in Figure 4.4.

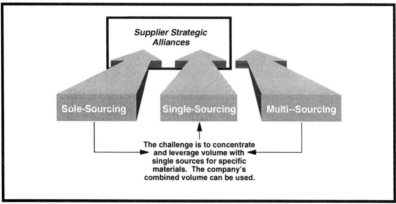

Figure 4.4

What type of sourcing do you use most in your company? Are there additional advantages and disadvantages you can identify for the type of sourcing you use most?

Type of Sourcing: _____
Additional Advantages

Additional Disadvantages

In terms of ways to minimize the risks detailed in the earlier section, below is a list of examples which have been used by many companies to reduce these risks.

- Utilize global value equation (not just price) to select sources (we address this in Chapter Five) .
- Plan on multi-year contracts.
- Write a "tight" supply agreement, with clear terms and conditions.
  - Period (e.g. 3 years)

- Volume differential (e.g. +/- 20% automatically included/covered)
- If natural disaster, then supplier agrees to supply resources (e.g. technology, labor, etc.) to alternative source of supply if necessary to keep purchaser's business in operation.
- If supplier disaster, then ... (same as above).
- If material becomes limited in supply due to supplier issues (e.g. yield) or market issues (e.g. increasing demand), the purchaser gets priority/right of first refusal to any material prior to allocation.
- If purchaser develops material which replaces said material, supplier will get opportunity to produce said material of acceptable quality, within x (e.g. 3 months) of when a specification and sample are provided; if supplier cannot produce, then purchaser has right to purchase material elsewhere.
- If competitive supplier develops and makes available material which replaces said material, and purchaser is interested in said material, contracted supplier will get opportunity ... (same as above).
- Agree to price for year one (1), with escalation/de-escalation formula tied to a published index.
- Use rice "escape clause" which takes into account competitive environment (e.g. tie to Chemical Week, which publishes price of many commodity-type chemicals).
- Cost savings/sharing will be passed through on a x%/x% (e.g. 50/50) basis, to take effect

on the first day of the month following when the change was implemented.

  – Disputes will be negotiated; if dispute cannot be successfully negotiated, then parties agree to nonbinding arbitration; each party will pay their own legal fees.

• Keep multiple suppliers qualified, so when a second/third source is required due to a supply interruption time does not have to be spent qualifying them.

• Balance single-sourcing among suppliers so you always have a "foot in the door" with alternative sources of supply where possible; an example is shown in Figure 4.5.

Strategic Sourcing Plans

A strategic sourcing plan is a written plan for a key material in a key market, one which meets the key market criteria we addressed above. Its purpose is to bring together the data gathering, analysis, and risk assessment intelligence into a concise, implementable recommendation which can be used to seek cross-functional and management concurrence to a path forward, and provide the "blueprint" to focus resources on the path forward.

While the plan itself is dependent on the selection criteria/global value equation we address in Chapter 5, for now we will address the elements that should be included in the plan and some sample wording for each element. For illustrative purposes, the examples are from a straightforward plan for sugar in the Northeast for a food company.

Material	Single Source	1st Back-Up Source	2nd Back-Up Source
Chemical 1	Supplier A	Supplier B	Supplier C
Chemical 2	Supplier B	Supplier C	Supplier D
Chemical 3	Supplier C	Supplier D	Supplier A
Chemical 4	Supplier D	Supplier A	Supplier B

Figure 4.5

The elements of a strategic sourcing plan include: recommendation, market review, discussion (overview, global value equation factors), award and risks, more aggressive alternative and risks, less aggressive alternative and risks, and who was involved in developing the plan. We will address each in turn.

Recommendation

The recommendation element is the "what" you recommend be done and what it means to the business (across multiple factors). For example: "contract for the period 1/1/xx through 12/31/xx for our (Plant) sugar (specifications 1, 2, and 3) requirements as follows:"

	%	MM Units	$K Volume
Supplier A	67	20.0	5,882
Supplier B	—	—	—
Supplier C	33	10.0	2,901
Totals		30.0	8,783

"This allocation saves $77K annually versus maintaining the current allocation and $119K versus pre-inquiry prices, and leaves $80K (51%) 'on the table.'" "On the table" refers to additional savings that could have been obtained by purchasing based on lowest price alone. This example is the financial factor. You should continue to give headlines on what it means for each factor in the global value equation important for this sourcing decision.

Market Review

There are four subelements usually contained in the market review element of the plan: 1) supply base, 2) last award, 3) market/requirement changes, and 4) pre-inquiry/award timing.

From a supply base standpoint, you should talk about who is available to do business with. For example: "Due to Supplier B's overwhelming dominance in the Northeast, Supplier Z when out of business a couple of years ago, and we are limited to Supplier B, Supplier A, and Supplier C as potential suppliers without paying substantial freight. As a result, we separately inquiry and contract for our requirements in the Northeast to lock in lower refining margins."

From a last award standpoint, you should review what you did during the last award period, and what has transpired since. For example: "For the 19xx through 19xx award period, we contracted with Supplier A for 25MM pounds, +/- 20% to be used at (Plant), and Supplier B for 20MM pounds, +/- 10% to be used at any (company) plants. Supplier C was not awarded business since it offered value equal to Supplier A's, and Supplier B was needed for specialty sugar requirements. By the end of calendar year 19xx, (company) will have taken the minimum amounts of 20MM pounds and 18MM pounds from both Supplier A and Supplier B, respectively. This was done consciously to minimize the amount of higher priced Supplier B sugar we had to utilize at other locations to meet our contract commitments."

From a market/requirement changes standpoint, you should review what is new and meaningful. For example: "In the last six months, there were significant market and requirement changes. Market changes included Coke and Pepsi formula changes toward more use of HFCS as a substitute for sugar. This move had a bigger impact on Northeast refiners since replacement business is difficult to obtain in this area. Requirement changes have eliminated the need to rely on Supplier B for our specialty sugar needs. For (Plant), Supplier C is qualified on both specifications 2 and 3, and Supplier A was qualified on specification 3 within the last month. At our other plants, (Plant) is grinding its own specification 4 sugar and (Plant) plans to do the same by the end of this calendar year. As backup, both Supplier D and Supplier E are qualified on this specification. In addition, (Plant) plans to grind its own specification 5 sugar by the end of this calendar year. As backup, Supplier F was qualified within the last six months. Supplier B is still the only qualified supplier of specification 6, free flowing brown sugar. Efforts to reformulate our products with brown sugar molasses are still underway but are proceeding slowly and are not expected to be completed prior to 19xx."

From a pre-inquiry/award timing standpoint, you should review anything unique about the timing of the inquiry or the award. For example: "Due to the Coke and Pepsi reformulations noted above and Supplier C's interest in getting some of (company's) business, we expected aggressive bidding. In addition to our written inquiry, pre-inquiry meetings were held with all three suppliers emphasizing our expectations. In terms of timing, we inquired and recommended contracting for our needs now because of the uncertainty of the successfulness of the reexport program. By contracting prior to its going into effect (estimated as July 1), we can lock in lower margins."

Discussion

There are two subelements usually contained in the discussion element of the plan: 1) an overview, and 2) a detailed discussion of the global value equation factors.

An overview is exactly what it sounds like, an overview. For example: "Of the three suppliers quoted, the nonincumbent Supplier C offers the best value. As shown in the recap on Attachment X, with the current #12 sugar price of $.xx/cwt., Supplier C's quote is $.xx/cwt. and $.xx/cwt. lower than the incumbents, Supplier A and Supplier B, respectively. Supplier A also submitted an aggressive quotation of $.xx/cwt. lower than last period's margin, while Supplier B increased its margin by $.xx/cwt." This example is the financial factor. You should continue to give an overview for each factor in the global value equation important for this sourcing decision. As mentioned earlier, we will address the global value equation in Chapter Five.

Award and Risks

The award element is the "what" you are awarding and why, and the risks associated with the award. For example: "The recommended purchasing plan in Option III on Attachment X was based primarily on Supplier A's minimum volume terms of 20MM pounds and the savings Supplier A offered. As noted above, this plan will save $77K versus maintaining the current allocation and $199K versus pre-inquiry prices." You should continue, and outline the risks associated with this award.

More Aggressive Alternative and Risks

The more aggressive alternative is an award alternative usually associated with more risk. You should explain what the more aggressive alternative is, and why it is not recommended. For example: "The recommended plan versus Option II, lowest cost source, leaves $80K (51% of the savings available) on the table. To further take advantage of this savings, Supplier A's business would have to be cut significantly. For example, if less than 20MM pounds are awarded to Supplier A, the refining margin increases $.xx/cwt. As a result, Supplier A's business would have to be cut to 13MM pounds just to break-even with the proposed purchasing plan. A shift in business of this magnitude is not warranted given the overall value this incumbent offers."

Less Aggressive Alternative and Risks

The less aggressive alternative is an award alternative usually associated with less risk. You should explain what the less aggressive alternative is, and why it is not recommended. For example: "A less aggressive plan would include an award for Supplier B and less of an award for Supplier C. Based on last period's feedback to both suppliers (i.e., Supplier B was informed it was not as competitive as others, and Supplier C was informed it needed to offer value better than the incumbents) a less aggressive plan would cause us to lose our credibility with both suppliers. Supplier B still has the opportunity to compete for business at our (Plant) and (Plant) facilities, and will continue to supply 633K pounds of brown sugar."

From this example, you can also see the importance of continuity and consistency of messages, i.e., knowing what has been said and done from period to period and in past sourcing plans.

Who Was Involved

Who was on the sourcing team and involved in developing the plan should be mentioned here. We address cross-functional sourcing teams in Chapter 5.

Best Practice Strategies

In conjunction with developing key market criteria and determining key markets, gathering external and internal data, deciding between sole- versus single- versus multi-sourcing, and writing sourcing plans, it is important to be aware of current and emerging best practice strategies. Ones we summarize for you here include: the pantry concept, fact-based negotiation, consortium buying, and facilitating strategic supplier relationships.

The pantry concept is simply maintaining a select set of consistent, reliable, ready-to-use materials to choose from for development or redesign of products sourced from a strategic supplier. Key benefits from this approach are reduced time to market for new products which are aligned with the strategic sourcing strategy, reduced downtime (improved manufacturability), improved finished goods quality, and reduced material inventory. This approach helps avoid both material and supplier proliferation.

Fact-based negotiation is a structured approach for analyzing, developing, and implementing strategic sourcing arrangements with suppliers. Some key principles and benefits are that it recognizes and utilizes powerful negotiating techniques, leverages a cross-functional team approach to negotiations, is fact-based and information driven, and ultimately leads to stronger relationships with fewer suppliers. Differences between the traditional negotiating process and the fact-based process, and the desired outcomes can be seen in Figure 4.6.

Consortium buying can be utilized in many instances to capitalize on greater buying or transportation leverage. It consists of purchasers from like suppliers from the same location. Membership is typically required in the consortium to be a participating party. Supplier negotiations are conducted by a consortium team, and significant benefits can be realized both in material cost savings as well as potential transportation savings. Reduced lead times, more frequent deliveries, and more on-time deliv-

Traditional Process	*Fact-Based Process*	*Desired Outcomes*
• Purchaser and supplier representative have a one-to-one relationship • Outcomes heavily impacted by personal dynamics and style • Objectivity difficult to maintain • Negotiations focused on single issue – price • Purchaser often reactive and lacks analytical support	• Comprehensive methodology • Purchaser and supplier represented by teams having an appropriate range of expertise • Outcomes dependent on data and facts presented • Objectivity promoted by multiple points of view • Negotiations address multiple issues – selection criteria/global value equation factors	• Neutralize any power imbalance • Eliminate "hidden" agendas from negotiations • Stronger relationship with fewer suppliers • Higher purchaser value

Figure 4.6

eries are also benefits frequently realized. Due to the nature of consortiums, it is usually for tactical buying and transaction-focused purchases.

Facilitating strategic supplier relationships starts with getting your internal house in order before visiting your supplier's house. For example, we suggest forming cross-functional sourcing teams, developing and tracking performance measures, aligning rewards with performance, growing skills through goal-based learning and other training methods, and having a communication strategy. We will address cross-functional sourcing teams in detail in Chapter Five.

Summary

In this chapter we addressed supply strategy. This included identifying key market criteria, gathering internal and external data, sole- versus single- versus multi-sourcing, strategic sourcing plans, and some best practice strategies. In several examples we mentioned selection criteria/global value equation and cross-functional sourcing teams. In Chapter Five, we address strategic sourcing, which includes both of these topics and identifying potential suppliers and rationalizing current suppliers.

Introduction

In this chapter we address the heart of supplier selection, strategic sourcing. This includes selection criteria or a global value equation, identifying potential suppliers, cross-functional sourcing teams, and rationalizing suppliers. A long list of potential selection criteria is shared, as well as a sample global value equation focused on: price, quality, service, technology, partnership, and globalization/localization. A value indexing methodology, which is an emerging best practice to develop, manage, and execute with cross-functional sourcing teams is shared. How to determine value indexing factors, establish guidelines and weights, and develop an operating system is covered, including an example from an electronics company.

Selection Criteria/Global Value Equation

Sourcing excellence depends on having a global value equation. Getting to a global value equation requires consideration of many different criteria, some of which can be "grouped" into factors. First, we will provide an extensive list of potential selection criteria. Second, we will address the global value equation.

In terms of potential selection criteria, the list from *Supplier Certification II: A Handbook for Achieving Excellence Through Continuous Improvement* by Peter L. Grieco, Jr. (PT Publications, Inc; West Palm Beach, FL) can be seen in Figure 5.1.

• Specifications	• Preventive Maintenance	• Customer Base
• Producibility	• Policies & Procedures	• On-Time Delivery
• Geographic Location	• Subcontractor Policy	• Tool Tracking
• Quality History	• Research & Development	• Smoking Policy
• Environmental Programs	• Self Assessment	• Ethics
• Facilities & Equipment	• Market Involvement	• Housekeeping
• Education & Training	• Capability	• Percent of Business
• Process & Quality Control	• Capacity	• Multiple Plants
• Competitive Pricing	• Financial Condition	• Calibration History
• Prior & Post Sales Support	• Quantity	• Six Sigma Program
• Knowledgeable Sales Force	• Labor Conditions	• Mgmt. Commitment
• Organization	• Cost Control	• ISO 9000/9002

Figure 5.1

What additional criteria can you think of that may have been considered by your company in the past?

_____

_____

_____

_____

While it is possible to select different criteria to use for every sourcing decision, that approach is not recommended for several reasons. First, it is difficult to align your criteria with your mission and objectives if the criteria is constantly changing. Second, it can become individual or group dependent, i.e., the criteria that is selected is determined more by other factors (e.g. hidden agenda, personality, dominate style, etc.) than the company's mission and objectives. Third, it is a very time consuming and laborious process to repeat over and over from scratch. And fourth, it results in sending mixed signals to suppliers and internal customers.

In order to overcome these drawbacks, we recommend you appoint a senior cross-functional team, called an Executive Steering Committee (ESC). One of the ESC's roles is to select the criteria that most aligns with your mission and objectives for a cross-section of materials, and "group" that criteria into factors which can be used universally in a global value equation. Later in this chapter we address weighting the factors. An example of "groupings" of criteria into a global value equation for an electronics company is shown in Figure 5.2.

Factors	Priority Criteria
Price	Net delivered, payment terms, currency valuations, usage and processing costs
Quality	Conformance to specifications, consistency within control limits, results of quality audits
Service	Lead times, on-time delivery performance, inventory, change-overs, responsiveness, information networking (e.g. EDI)
Technology	Performance, proprietarymtechnology, exclusivity options and length, responsiveness to request for specification changes
Partnership	Long-term viability of supplier alignment with value proposition (mission/objectives), business case (cost/benefit, risk analysis), lenght of relationship (history)
Globalization/ Localization	Monoploy risk, proximity to using facilities, availability to third party (e.g. government) funding

Figure 5.2

Using the list of potential selection criteria, including your additions, list all the criteria you think best aligns with your company's mission and objectives:

_____   _____   _____

_____   _____   _____

_____   _____   _____

_____   _____   _____

Next, look for logical groupings of criteria, and enter all the "like" criteria in the first space of the "Priority Criteria" column in Figure 5.2a. Cross out the criteria on the list above as you enter the criteria in Figure 5.2a. Continue with the second, third, etc. spaces until all your criteria have been entered once. Discipline yourself to look for no more than six logical groupings. After you have completed this, look for "themes" for each section of criteria groupings, and enter that theme in the "Factor" column.

Factors	Priority Criteria

Figure 5.2a

After this has been completed, you should write a short description for each priority criteria within a factor so there is no misunderstanding about what is being sought and evaluated. Three examples of descriptions are:

- **Lead Time** – Lead time is the amount of elapsed time required from placement of a purchase order to delivery of materials. (Note: For your firm you may chose to define lead time as the amount of elapsed time required from the release of material to delivery of materials, i.e., your inventory policy needs to be reflected.)

- **On-Time Delivery Performance** – On-time delivery performance is the percentage of material that was delivered at the requested time. Neither early or late deliveries are considered "on-time." (Note: "Time" should be defined more specifically for your company. For example, it may be the day you requested, window of shift times you specified, or a specific dock time that was assigned.)

For example, at a consumer products company delivery performance was defined as:

- **On-Time** - Delivery on the exact date requested and within plus or minus 15 minutes of the designated dock time
- **Early** – Delivery on a date before requested and/or earlier than 15 minutes of the designated dock time
- **Late** – Delivery on a date after requested and/or later than 15 minutes of the designated dock time

To determine the percentage of on-time, early, and late deliveries, consider the following sample portion of a receiving recap for Supplier A during the month of September:

Amount Req'd & Rec'd	Date Requested	Time Requested	Date Received	Time Received	Results
1,000,000	Sept. 1	2:00 p.m.	Sept. 1	2:15 p.m.	On-Time
1,000,000	Sept. 14	11:00 a.m.	Sept. 14	1:00 p.m.	Late
500,000	Sept. 20	10:00 a.m.	Sept. 20	11:00 a.m.	Late
1,000,000	Sept. 27	2:00 p.m.	Sept. 26	9:00 a.m.	Early
3,500,000					

% On-Time	=	1,000,000/3,500,000	=	28.6%
% Early	=	1,000,000/3,500,000	=	28.6%
% Late	=	1,500,000/3,500,000	=	42.8%
Total	=			100.0%

As you can see in this example, the delivery performance is weighted by the quantity. This is important due to the impact of quantity on production needs and inventory levels, i.e., the bigger the quantity, the bigger the impact. Therefore, it is not recommended you treat all deliveries as equal and count the number of deliveries on-time, early, and late. However, this latter approach is a faster and easier way to get started if you are doing nothing at your company today. Also, please note that quantity performance is not the same thing as delivery performance, i.e., "match," "exceed," and "short" are separate performance measures relative to the amounts received versus the amounts requested.

Using the consumer product company's definitions of delivery performance and referencing the example above, compute the percentage for on-time, early, and late for the information provided below:

Amount Req'd & Rec'd	Date Requested	Time Requested	Date Received	Time Received	Results
900,000	Sept. 1	2:00 p.m.	Sept. 2	9:00 a.m.	_____
1,000,000	Sept. 14	11:00 a.m.	Sept. 14	10:45 a.m.	_____
500,000	Sept. 20	10:00 a.m.	Sept. 20	11:00 a.m.	_____
800,000	Sept. 23	2:00 p.m.	Sept. 22	2:00 p.m.	_____
400,000	Sept. 27	2:00 p.m.	Sept. 27	1:45 p.m.	_____

% On-Time = _____ = ____ %
% Early   = _____ = ____ %
% Late   = _____ = ____ %

Total   =   100%

- **Length of Relationship (History)** - Length of relationship is the number of months the supplier has been shipping product to your company. This history provides the basis to determine the supplier's "As Is" performance.

Using the examples above, write descriptions for two of the priority criteria you identified for your company:

- _____
  _____
  _____
  _____

- _____
  _____
  _____
  _____

After the criteria are defined, the factors need to be weighted. This is part of the value indexing methodology which is presented in the Cross-Functional Sourcing Teams section.

Identifying Potential Suppliers

Identifying potential suppliers is a process limited only by your imagination and initiative. The ways to identify potential suppliers can be characterized as passive or proactive.

Passive Identification - Despite connotations of the word "passive," this is the most important type of identification of potential suppliers since it generates a list of suppliers who want your business the most. Passive identification includes generating a list from:

• who you are buying from now,

- who else you have "qualified" to buy from (e.g. back-up sources),

- who is in the qualification process,

- who has contacted you to interest you in buying from them,

- suppliers you are buying "like" materials from, and

- other suppliers which have been brought to your attention through other functions (e.g. Product Development, Operations, and Engineering).

Proactive Identification - Despite connotations of the word "proactive," this type of identification generates longer shots and is generally more risky than passive identification. At the same time, however, it is more likely to uncover new technologies, next generation materials, and new suppliers than passive identification. Proactive identification includes generating a list from:

- establishing and utilizing Listening Posts for supplier referrals,

- asking other people in Procurement and other functions (e.g. Product Development, Operations, and Engineering) for supplier ideas,

- contacting professional societies,

- using the Thomas Register, and

- using other "buyer guides."

Listening Posts are formal points (e.g. e-mail address, mail drop, phone extension, etc.) established for receipt of input at multiple geographic locations. Once established, the Posts are widely publicized throughout your firm as a way for any employee to get a good supplier idea into the supplier selection process.

You are probably thinking that one risk with this approach is supplier proliferation. That is certainly a risk that needs to be managed, as we discussed when we introduced the pantry concept in Chapter Four. The reality, of course, is that some suppliers need to be rationalized because of poor performance, outdated technology, or a host of other reasons. You may need and want to bring a new supplier on board, while you reduce your overall supplier base. We will address this further in the Rationalizing Suppliers section.

Cross-Functional Sourcing Teams

As noted, the first cross-functional team you need to appoint is an Executive Steering Committee to: 1) select the criteria that most aligns with your mission and objectives for a cross-section of materials, and 2) "group" that criteria into factors which can be used universally in a global value equation. If you are organized by process, representatives from the "fulfill demand" process should be selected for the cross-functional team. If you are organized by function, the functions usually sought for representatives include Procurement, Operations, Product Development, and Engineering. Other functions often selected, depending on the approach to quality at your company, include Technical Services and Quality Assurance. Less often, Finance and Sales are also included.

The process to identify, select, and reach consensus on the priority criteria is usually difficult and complex, and requires a skilled facilitator. We recommend you contract with an expert.

After the global value equation is determined, weight guidelines should be established by the Executive Steering Committee for groups of "like" items. For example, referring back to the types of purchases we defined in Chapter Three, ingredients/raw materials, packaging materials, MRO supplies, equipment and capital, contractors and services, and utilities may each have their own set of weight guidelines. Or, a subgrouping of types of purchases, like food ingredients, chemicals, and so forth may have their own set of weight guidelines. However, it is important not to have weight guidelines for each material. Discipline yourself to establish the highest common denominator possible for "like" items. Once the weight guidelines are established, they should be given to the sourcing teams.

Cross-Functional Sourcing Teams (CFSTs) should consist of representatives from the same process or functions from which the Executive Steering Committee was established. CFSTs should only be established for the same materials for which you wrote strategic sourcing plans. As noted in Chapter Four, a strategic sourcing plan is a written plan for a key material in a key market. As such, a CFST is a cross-functional team established to source (select suppliers) for a key material in a key market. Their orders of business are:

1) The CFST should familiarize themselves with the strategic sourcing plan for this material, and up-

date relevant sections (e.g. Market/Requirement Changes). This will require the CFST to: know their customers; understand their customers' needs; review customers' expectations; determine volume/services required and timing; develop inquiry objectives/expectations with their customers; and determine the value of the inquiry versus contract extension, negotiation, spot buying, and so forth. In most cases, "customers" refers to internal customers (e.g. Operations).

Some reasons to inquiry and some reasons not to inquiry are shown in Figure 5.3.

2) Agree on the exact weights that will be utilized to source the key material. The exact weights the CFST agrees on must fall within the factor weight ranges established by the Executive Steering Committee. This leeway allows for some tailoring, but not so much that the drawbacks of not aligning with your mission and objectives, becoming individual or group dependent, spending a lot of time on a repetitive process, and sending mixed signals come into play.

3) Gather and analyze historical information to determine the suppliers' "As Is" performances.

4) Identify potential suppliers for the key material.

5) Conduct the inquiry, which can be done in many ways and will often include meetings, site visits, and so forth.

6) Analyze the results of the inquiry, enter a number representative of the quote and information for each factor in the value indexing matrix, rank

Reasons To Inquiry	Reasons Not To Inquiry
• Currently have more than one supplier • Think single source of supply is not providing total value you want • Want to change supplier(s) • Fairly standardized materials and/or technology • Market conditions are stable • Material and/or quantity requirements have changed and are known • Think negotiation option(s) would add little value versus objectives • Want to create competitive conditions or make an intervention	• Currently only have one supplier and are not willing to change • Are sole-sourced • Unique/custom material and/or technology (e.g. under patent) • Scarce industry supply • Rapidly rising pricing conditions • Material and/or quantity requirements are not defined • Just want to find out where single-sourced supplier's price stands, but aren't willing to move business (e.g. benchmark)

Figure 5.3

the numbers against one another (e.g. Supplier A - 2, Supplier B - 1, and Supplier C - 3), compute the value for each supplier for each factor (CFST weight multiplied by rank or 30% x 2 = .60), and total the value for each supplier. This is shown in Figure 5.4.

7) Discuss the total values, merits of sole-, single-, and multi-sourcing in this situation, and agree on supplier selection and allocation (e.g. Supplier A - 100% or Supplier A - 60% and Supplier B - 40%).

8) Revise strategic sourcing plan to reflect recommendation.

9) Present strategic sourcing plan to Executive Steering Committee; seek approval.

GVE Factor	Guideline Weight	CFST Weight	Supplier A			Supplier B			Supplier C		
			Quote	Rank	Value	Quote	Rank	Value	Quote	Rank	Value
Price	20-30%	30%	11.25	2	0.60	10.71	1	0.30	11.75	3	0.90
Quality	20-30%	20%	90	2	0.40	80	3	0.60	95	1	0.20
Service	20-30%	30%	3	1	0.30	4	2	0.60	6	3	0.90
Technology	5-10%	5%	50	1	0.05	50	1	0.05	50	1	0.05
Partnership	5-20%	10%	50	3	0.30	75	2	0.20	100	1	0.10
Global/Local	5-10%	5%	75	2	0.10	100	1	0.05	50	3	0.15
Totals		100%			1.75			1.80			2.30

Figure 5.4

In this example, Supplier A offers the best overall value according to the Global Value Equation (GVE) and should get all or most of the business.

A variation of this value indexing methodology is called Supplier Value Added (SVA). SVA is "the relative value attributed to a supplier for providing competitive advantage." At AT&T it is utilized to examine the aspects of suppliers' goods or services that create value. An example of a Supplier SVA Scorecard from "Managing Supplier Value Added" by Daniel J. Carroll, Jr. from a Conference Board report is shown in Figure 5.5.

The supplier management principles AT&T utilizes throughout this process are:

- Supply and technology strategies are driven by business objectives.
- You and your supplier can achieve more through shared expectations than adversarial relationships.
- You and your supplier are open and honest with each other and are willing to work together to achieve mutual business advantages from a relationship.

| Supplier: Supplier A | | | Period: 3 Q 97 | | |
| Commodity: XYZ | | | Region: ABC | | |

Weight	Element Measurement	Score	Weight	Performance	Contribution
25%	**Quality/Reliability**			66%	16.5%
	Quality performance	21%	43%		
	Receiving inspection performance	100%	34%		
	Field retrofits required	100%	23%		
25%	**Delivery/Flexibility**			89%	22.2%
	On-time committed receipt date	96%	43%		
	Delivery error performance	100%	34%		
	Flexibility and lead time	58%	23%		
25%	**Technology**			73%	18.2%
	Access to technology	73%	80%		
	Technology roadmap match	75%	20%		
15%	**Service**			76%	11.4%
	Purchasing/Materials support	78%	65%		
	EDI capability support	100%	15%		
	Leading-edge procurement support	50%	20%		
10%	**Environment**			100%	10.0%
	Environmental considerations	100%	100%		
	Performance Rating	(Goal = 100%)			78.3%
	Total Cost of Ownership			85%	100.0%
75%	Purchase price	93%	75%		
5%	Contracting costs	60%	5%		
5%	Order processing costs	75%	5%		
5%	Import/export costs	90%	5%		
10%	Correction costs	100%	10%		
	Cost Rating	(Goal = 100%)			85.1%
	SVA Score = 70% (Performance) + 30% (TCO) =				80.3%

Figure 5.5 – Source: "Strategic Purchasing: Sourcing for the Bottom Line," The Conference Board, Report No. 1157-96-CH, ©1996.

- Performance is measured and reviewed with the suppliers on a regular basis.
- Both you and your supplier strive for continuous improvement to deliver maximum value to the end customer.
- Decisions should be based on facts.

Rationalizing Suppliers

In Chapter Three, we addressed situation analysis, including how to establish a baseline of the "As Is" situation. Part of the profile of purchases included determining the percentage of suppliers making up 80% of the purchase expenditures (the 80/20 Rule). In order to establish this percentage, you need to have determined the number of suppliers you have. Figure 5.6 shows an example of an "As Is" base of 692 suppliers.

Reducing the supply base results in significant benefits, including: leveraging volume, focusing resources, reducing administrative overhead, providing the basis for supplier strategic alliances, getting more return for your investments (e.g. molds, EDI, etc.), and becoming the purchaser of choice. The company in this example wanted to reduce their supply base to 395, which represents a 43% reduction. The "As Is" versus "To Be" by purchase type is shown in Figure 5.7.

Using Figures 5.5 and 5.6 as examples, indicate the number of "As Is" suppliers by type of purchases at your company. Then, based on what you know, identify a "To Be" goal for each, and compute the percent reduction the "To Be" number represents.

	# Suppliers	
	"As Is"	"To Be"
Ingredients/Raw Materials	_____	_____
Packaging Materials	_____	_____
MRO Supplies	_____	_____
Equipment & Capital	_____	_____

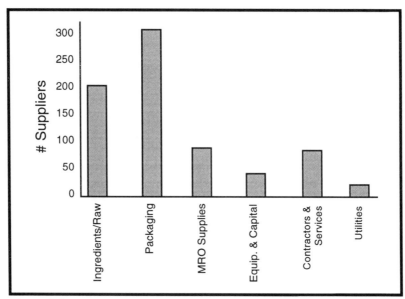

Figure 5.6

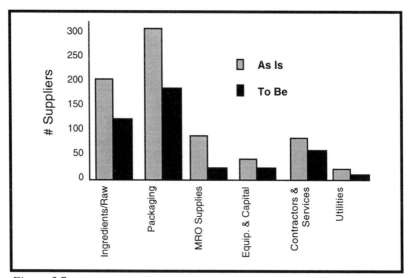

Figure 5.7

Contractors & Services	_____	_____
Utilities	_____	_____
Totals	_____	_____
% Reduction	**Base**	_____

Given the size of the reduction in our example (43%), we recommend developing interim reduction goals along a time line. An illustration of this is shown in Figure 5.8.

Some people call rationalizing suppliers "firing" suppliers; we do not recommend using this term. Firing has a connotation of nonperformance, when in fact you may eliminate suppliers over time who are performing acceptably, but still do not represent the best overall value versus other suppliers you chose to retain. You never want to burn bridges with suppliers you eliminate, and "firing" them will leave a very negative taste in their mouths which will last a long time.

Metal Can Case

One of the objectives of achieving material objectives at a consumer products company is through "the fair use and encouragement of competition." In doing so, their policy states that they will take business from an active supplier (an incumbent) only for good reason. "The offering of equivalent value by others, in and of itself, does not provide reason to take business away from the current supplier." Work through the following case, which requires using some of the information presented in this chapter.

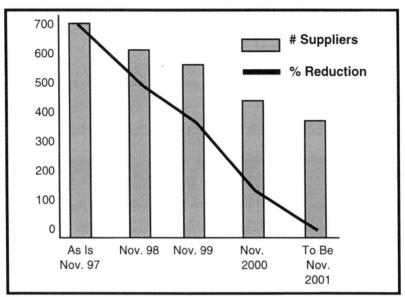

Figure 5.8

Background

For the past 24 months, the metal can industry has been steadily raising prices to offset increases in the cost of labor, energy, steel, etc. This is done in the same fashion as steel industry price hikes, where an industry leader announces an increase and the others follow suit. Most can manufacturers sell against a list price, unless competition is present. With competition, the prices are likely to be 15-25% under list.

It is customary to inquiry and award can requirements by plant, by size. Suppliers A & B are currently supplying your one pound coffee can requirements at (Plant), as well as participating in coffee and shortening business at your other plants. Prior to B's arrival on the scene several years ago, you had been buying from A at list prices. The response to your recent inquiry (which did not include Supplier C) showed no change in the one pound (Plant) situation, and you awarded the business as follows:

Supplier A: 20MM cans at $120.00/K for a 15MM can minimum (A is a high quality, excellent service company)

Supplier B: 30MM cans at $110.00/K for a 20MM can minimum (B's quality and service is below average across the board)

Scenario 1

Several months later, Supplier C, a quality shortening can supplier, expressed interest in the (Plant) one pound business and indicated their current price would be $105.00/K. Based on this you began a lengthy qualification (which A & B were aware of), and upon completion of the qualification and about three months before the end of the previous award period you inquiried the business (50MM) with the following results (there had been no changes in supplier input costs):

Supplier A: $105.00/K at 15MM minimum (vs. $120.00/K current per above)

Supplier B: $ 95.00/K at 20MM minimum (vs. $110.00/K current per above)

Supplier C: $105.00/K at 5MM minimum (vs. $105.00/K at start of qualification)

How would you allocate the business?

Supplier	Quoted Price	Award Quantity	Award Cost	Comments/Reasoning
A	$105.00/K	_____	_____	_____
B	$ 95.00/K	_____	_____	_____
C	$105.00/K	_____	_____	_____
Total =		50MM	_____	Left On Table = _____

Overall Comments/Reasoning:

_____

_____

Scenario 2

How would you allocate the business if the inquiry results were:

Supplier A: $100.00/K at 15MM minimum (vs. $120.00/K current per above)

Supplier B: $ 95.00/K at 20MM minimum (vs. $110.00/K current per above)

Supplier C: $105.00/K at 5MM minimum (vs. $105.00/K at start of qualification)

Supplier	Quoted Price	Award Quantity	Award Cost	Comments/Reasoning
A	$100.00/K	_____	_____	_____
B	$ 95.00/K	_____	_____	_____
C	$105.00/K	_____	_____	_____
Total =		50MM	_____	Left On Table = _____

Overall Comments/Reasoning:

_____

_____

General Questions

What, if any, justification is there for awarding business to Supplier C?

_____

_____

_____

If C's presence in the market has resulted in savings to your company, should C benefit? If so, are you being fair to the incumbents?

_____

_____

_____

How does your desire to single-source where possible impact your decisions?

_____

_____

_____

Was qualifying Supplier C mid-award period without the effort being kicked off by an inquiry a smart move? What would you do different, if anything?

_____

_____

_____

Summary

In this chapter we addressed the heart of supplier selection, strategic sourcing. This included selection criteria or a global value equation, identifying potential suppliers, cross-functional sourcing teams, and rationalizing suppliers. A long list of potential selection criteria was shared, as well as an example global value equation focused on price, quality, service, technology, partnership, and globalization/localization. A value indexing methodology, which is an emerging best practice to develop, manage, and execute with cross-functional sourcing teams was shared, along with a Supplier Value Added (SVA) example from AT&T. And, a case was presented for you to utilize some of the information included in this chapter.

TACTICAL
BUYING &
ELECTRONIC
COMMERCE

CHAPTER SIX

Introduction

In this chapter we address tactical buying and electronic commerce. This includes differences versus sourcing and identifying what is "new" about tactical buying that needs to be considered in supplier selection, the why and how to consolidate volume, centralized versus decentralized procurement, blanket orders, procurement cards, Electronic Data Interchange (EDI), intranets, and the Internet. In light of consolidating volume and reducing the supply base, the benefits of centralized, decentralized, and combination organizations from a procurement standpoint are reviewed. And "work-arounds," or alternatives when an organization is decentralized, are provided.

Differences Versus Sourcing

As noted in Chapter Three, tactical buying is focused on transactions and nonstrategic material buying. As such, it is closely aligned with the "ordering" portion of executing the purchasing transactions process. Both the exposure and relative power of suppliers are low. And, while multi-sourcing is the dominate type of sourcing utilized, the trend is toward single-sourcing in order to leverage volume.

Some elements of strategic sourcing included in Chapter Five also apply to tactical buying, but many do not and, if utilized, will result in wasting resources and "over buying." The elements which apply include the global value equation and rationalizing suppliers. The elements which generally do not apply include strategic sourcing plans, Cross-Functional Sourcing Teams (CFSTs), and elaborate or complex value indexing matrices or supplier SVA scorecards.

The Global Value Equation (GVE) is a company-wide equation which doesn't change by type of purchase. The Executive Steering Committee, when setting the weighting guidelines by type of material, will generally weight the price-related GVE factor heavily. For example, most MRO supplies should be bought tactically, with an emphasis on obtaining the lowest total cost possible.

As noted in Chapter Five, rationalizing suppliers and reducing the supply base results in significant benefits, including leveraging volume, focusing resources, reducing administrative overhead, and getting more return for your investments (e.g. EDI).

Consolidating Volume

Consolidating volume is all about leverage. A sourcing guideline regarding leverage in a Fortune 30 company includes the following key points:

- There is an opportunity to gain true competitive advantage by leveraging
- In decentralized organization, leveraging is a major challenge
- There is a dilution factor of acquiring in-depth supplier and market expertise – leveraging serves to offset this dilution.
- Leveraging means seeking out and taking advantage of opportunities available from total corporate knowledge, resources, strength, and diversity.
- The opportunities include:
  - sharing knowledge.
  - consolidating purchase volume in a way to enhance the value.
  - building on our successful supplier relationships in new situations.
  - seeking and replacing best approaches.

Competitive advantage through leveraging is clearly an opportunity as well as a challenge. It is vital that we seek out and help build appropriate leveraging mechanisms. Developing these systems and putting them to use will permit us to pursue and execute in optimum fashion leveraging opportunities that will provide our businesses with a major competitive advantage.

To illustrate how consolidating volume and leveraging work, assume you work in a multi-plant environment. In the "As Is," every plant is buying its own MRO supplies from different suppliers. An example for bearing purchases is shown in Figure 6.1.

Now, assume you rationalize suppliers, and designate one approved supplier for each major category of MRO supplies (e.g. bearings). In the "Interim," every plant is buying its own MRO supplies from the same, approved supplier. An example for bearing purchases is shown in Figure 6.2.

Next, assume you consolidate volume for all plants and negotiate a national contract with the approved supplier. In the "To Be," every plant releases its own MRO supplies from the same, approved supplier, against the same, national contract. An example for bearing purchases is shown in Figure 6.3.

In this bearings example, the "To Be" consolidated volume scenario nets $2.5K in annual savings. The potential savings of repeating this process across hundreds and potentially thousands of SKUs of MRO supplies is obviously significant.

Consider how your company currently buys MRO supplies. Is it more like Figure 6.1, Figure 6.2, or Figure 6.3? If it is more like Figure 6.1 or Figure 6.2, identify the top six categories of MRO supplies you think are the best candidates for consolidating volume in your company.

Plant	Supplier	Volume	Price	Average Monthly Cost	Projected Annual Cost
A	G	1,000	$0.20	$200	$2,400
B	H	300	$0.26	$ 78	$ 936
C	I	500	$0.24	$120	$1,440
D	J	200	$0.27	$ 54	$ 648
E	K	400	$0.25	$100	$1,200
F	L	700	$0.22	$154	$1,848
Totals		3,100	$0.23	$706	$8,472

Figure 6.1

Plant	Supplier	Volume	Price*	Average Monthly Cost	Projected Annual Cost
A	G	1,000	$0.20	$200	$2,400
B	G	300	$0.25	$ 75	$ 900
C	G	500	$0.22	$110	$1,320
D	G	200	$0.26	$ 52	$ 624
E	G	400	$0.24	$ 96	$1,152
F	G	700	$0.21	$147	$1,764
Totals		3,100	$0.22	$680	$8,160
Savings				$ 26	$ 312
* Assumes G has slightly lower list prices than Suppliers H-L					

Figure 6.2

1. _____   4. _____
2. _____   5. _____
3. _____   6. _____

Centralized Versus Decentralized

A centralized organization structure is generally one where a Procurement function exists in a headquarters location and sources and buys for the entire company, regardless of business unit, geography, or produc-

Plant	Supplier	Volume	Price*	Average Monthly Cost	Projected Annual Cost
A	G	1,000	$0.16	$160	$1,920
B	G	300	$0.16	$ 48	$ 576
C	G	500	$0.16	$ 80	$ 960
D	G	200	$0.16	$ 32	$ 384
E	G	400	$0.16	$ 64	$ 768
F	G	700	$0.16	$112	$1,344
Totals		3,100	$0.16	$496	$5,952
Savings				$210	$ 2,520
* Assumes G's price for quantities > 3,000 = $0.16					

Figure 6.3

ing facility. Key advantages of this structure are economies of scale, specialization, coordination, and control. Key drawbacks are market understanding, speed, and flexibility. An example of a centralized organization is shown in Figure 6.4.

A decentralized organization structure is generally one where a Procurement function exists in each business unit, geography, and/or producing facility and is co-located with the unit it supports. Key advantages of this structure are flexibility and market responsiveness. Key drawbacks are coordination, control, and efficiency. An example of a decentralized organization is shown in Figure 6.5.

A combination of a centralized and decentralized organization is a matrix organization, where a Procurement function exists at both the company and business unit (or geography or plant facility) levels, and has dual reporting relationships to both the business and the function. Key advantages of this structure are economies of scale, specialization, coordination, control, flexibility,

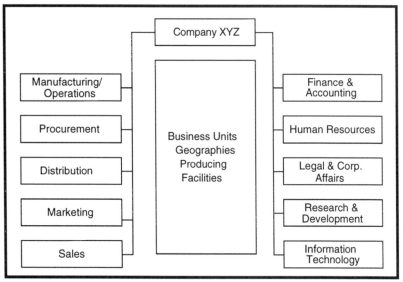

Figure 6.4

and market responsiveness. Key drawbacks are dual reporting relationships, conflicting priorities, and spread and cost of resources. An example of a matrix organization is shown in Figure 6.6.

The centralized organization structure (Figure 6.4) is functionally-oriented, and often results in "functional silos." The decentralized organization structure (Figure 6.5) and matrix organization structure (Figure 6.6) are more business-unit oriented but maintain the functions. None of these structures are process-oriented.

A process-oriented structure is one which involves major business processes. In the consumer products industry there are four major processes it must manage well: 1) develop products and processes, 2) generate demand, 3) fulfill demand, and 4) plan and manage

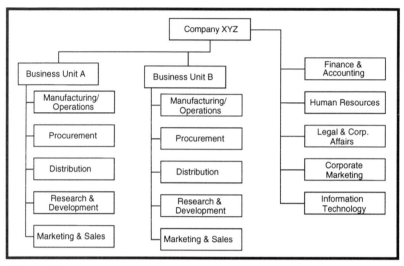

Figure 6.5

enterprise. Key advantages of this structure are a clear "line-of-sight" to customers, fewer non-valued-added activities, fewer resources, and greater ability to anticipate and respond to market changes. Key drawbacks are complexity and implementation challenges. An example of a process-oriented organization is shown in Figure 6.7.

Examples of companies which have implemented some form of a process-oriented organization include:

Merck – created a process-based organization to shift emphasis from a traditional research and development focus to customer-focused "pharmaceutical solutions."

Levi – developed a vision to achieve preeminent customer service by designing an end-to-end process for creating "ready-to-sell" products for unique and changing customer segments.

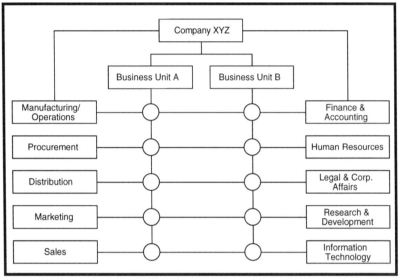

Figure 6.6

Cannon – realigned its internal processes to become an integrated "document services" provider to convey a consistent global quality and service image.

KFC – standardized store operations around ten core processes and defined a small set of key measures to improve quality, service, and cleanliness targets.

From a consolidating volume standpoint, it is significantly easier in centralized and process-oriented organization structures to consolidate and leverage volume, more difficult in a matrix organization structure, and most difficult in a decentralized organization structure. Regardless of the type of structure in your company, you need to find a way to consolidate and leverage volume to the greatest extent possible. Potential "work-arounds," or alternatives when the organization is decentralized include:

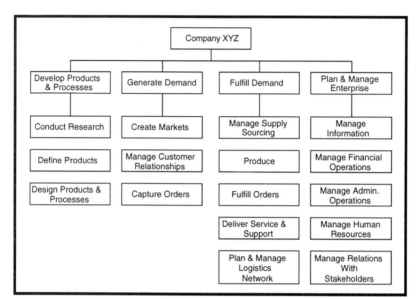

Figure 6.7

- Use the situation analysis we addressed in Chapter Three as a place to start. For example, in the profile of purchases by "to" location (Figure 3.11), start with the 10% of materials serving three plant locations. Make a business case for consolidation. Next, look at the 22% of materials serving two plant locations. Last, look at the 68% of materials serving one location and see where SKUs are identical or substitutes. Early wins are critical, i.e., success breeds success.

- Rationalize suppliers and designate one approved supplier for each major category of MRO supplies. In the "Interim," every plant is buying its own MRO supplies from the same, approved supplier. Reference the example in Figure 6.2.

- Consolidate volume for all plants and negotiate a national contract with the approved supplier. In the "To Be," every plant releases its own MRO supplies from the same approved supplier, against the same national contract. Refer to the example in Figure 6.3.

- Implement an enterprise-wide technology solution which enables volume consolidation with preapproved suppliers.

What type of organization structure exists in your company? Is it centralized, decentralized, matrix, or process-oriented? Based on your structure and the advantages and drawbacks noted for each, use the example "work-arounds" to consolidate volume in decentralized organizations to identify three additional alternatives you see to consolidate volume in your company.

Type of Organization Structure: _____
Additional Alternatives To Consolidate Volume:

1) _____

2) _____

3) _____

Blanket Orders

Blanket orders are a type of purchase order with a supplier at predetermined prices over a predetermined period of time (usually one or two years). Quantity is usually estimated with a range (e.g. 1MM units plus or minus 20%) in order to have negotiated and received most-favored customer prices. Blanket orders are utilized to reduce the number of small orders, utilizing short-term releases to satisfy demand requirements instead.

In the example represented in Figure 6.3 where you consolidated the volume for all plants and negotiated a national contract with the approved supplier, one blanket order would generally be written for plants to release their needs against. All invoices are issued against the blanket order number. When the period expires, the blanket order is terminated, unless you and supplier jointly agree to extend the period.

Procurement Cards

Like blanket orders, procurement cards are targeted at reducing the transaction costs of tactical buying. Specifically, procurement cards are designed to save companies the time and cost of small-dollar purchases, defined as $1K or less per purchase/invoice. In a 1995 survey, Gunn Partners found that purchases under $1K typically represent more than 70% of the transactions but less than 5% of the purchase dollars. For example, an ITT division's MRO invoices account for 59% of its manufacturing units invoice volume but less than 5% of the total purchase dollars. And, 81% of its MRO invoices are less than $1K, accounting for 3% of total spending. U.S. companies spend an estimated $300B annually on low-dollar volume purchases, representing 45-65% of all business orders but account for only 2-3% of total purchase dollars.

Unlike blanket orders, procurement cards are most effective when there are many suppliers. As shown in Figure 6.8, many small purchases are with once-a-year suppliers, requiring a lot of administrative time to set up and maintain accounts. Only 12% are used "regularly," or over 12 times per year.

How does a procurement card program work? It works essentially the same as a private credit card, except that multiple cards are issued to an organization for its employees to make business purchases (primarily MRO supplies) less than or equal to $1K. An employee buys items directly from suppliers (usually approved or designated suppliers), and the supplier sends an electronic invoice to the company's account payables department indicating the item, purchase amount, name of the employee, and the account the funds should be drawn from. The accounting department makes one monthly electronic payment to the purchase card organization.

Before implementing a procurement card program, companies usually designate:

- what can be purchased with the card,
- which suppliers should be used,
- the number of transactions allowed within a period (e.g. month),
- the amount of spending allowed within a period (e.g. month),
- the maximum spending limit for an item (e.g. $1K),
- how sales tax will be handled, and
- the process for post-purchase audits.

Fees for a procurement card vary from zero to $25 each annually. The leading providers of cards are MasterCard, Visa, and American Express. However, bank

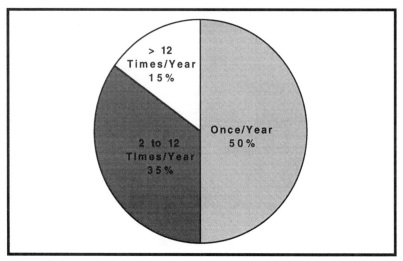

Figure 6.8

cards almost always need to be arranged through a money-center bank. American Express offers service directly: (800) 433-3550. Each procurement card program can be customized.

Estimates of companies currently using procurement cards range from 13% for all companies to 25% for companies with revenues exceeding $500MM annually. The projections for procurement card usage in the future range from 33% to 43%, respectively.

Two examples of companies utilizing procurement card programs and some of their results are recapped below:

- **Westinghouse Electric** – Westinghouse has an estimated 267K transactions worth $1B of total value annually. They determined 57% of the transactions were less than $500, and that the average order was $174. Westinghouse implemented a procurement card program, and saved $180 per invoice-processing transaction, reducing the total cost of order processing from $208 to $28 (87%).

- **Pepsi Cola** – Pepsi has an estimated 1.5MM invoices from 150K suppliers annually. They determined 35% of the transactions accounted for only 5% of the purchase dollars. Pepsi implemented a procurement card program, and by the end of 1994 management estimated total savings of $70-75MM, and 94% (234 of 250) accounts payable positions were able to be eliminated.

Additional benefits of procurement card programs include reduced cycle time, less inventory, increased cash flow, improved budget management, and less procurement resources required for tactical buying.

Does your company have a procurement card program? If so, what benefits have been realized by using the cards? If not, what next steps need to be taken to develop a business case for a procurement card program?

Procurement Card Program? _____
If yes, what benefits have been realized? If no, what next steps need to be taken?

1) _____

2) _____

3) _____

4) _____

5) _____

Electronic Commerce (E-commerce)

Electronic commerce (E-commerce) is defined by Andersen Consulting as "an interchange of goods, services, or property of any kind, between companies through an electronic medium." Historically, the electronic medium has been EDI. Today, it includes intranets and the Internet. You can think about this transformation in three waves, as shown in Figure 6.9.

From a buying standpoint, time, place, and form are becoming irrelevant, and the economics of doing business are being driven continually lower. The marketplace is being turned into marketspace.

Electronic Data Interchange (EDI)

In 1996, United States companies were estimated to have completed more than $300B worth of transactions using electronic data interchange (EDI) over value-added networks (VANs). While using VANs is usually associated with EDI, a company does not have to use a VAN to do EDI. All electronic transactions are recommended to use the American National Standards Institute (ANSI) X.12 standards. The X.12 standards are very flexible in order to accommodate multiple industries; however, the forms are broad (e.g. 1K items in formatting a purchase order). As a result, in a number of industry guidelines have been adopted to narrow approximately 90% of the options.

Benefits of EDI include reducing transaction costs, reducing cycle time, reducing inventories, and sharing point-of-sale (POS) and forecasting information.

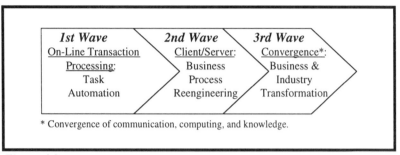

1st Wave	2nd Wave	3rd Wave
On-Line Transaction Processing: Task Automation	Client/Server: Business Process Reengineering	Convergence*: Business & Industry Transformation

* Convergence of communication, computing, and knowledge.

Figure 6.9

An example of one company which has benefited from using EDI is Avex Electronics. They have 30 major suppliers with whom they use EDI transactions, covering approximately 33% of their invoice process. It enabled them to reduce their accounts payable staff by 50%. In addition, Avex increased inventory turns and reduced Days Sales Outstanding (DSOs).

Another company doing business over EDI is Diamond Shamrock, who purchased National Convenience Stores (NCS) in the mid-1990s. Diamond Shamrock has been using EDI since 1989 over VANs. However, the company is also utilizing Chase Manhattan Bank via the Internet to issue electronic checks. The cost has been reduced from $2.00 for cutting a check manually to $.75 for an electronic check. Just taking into account the utility invoices from over 1500 retail convenience and gas stores outlets (C-Stores and G-Stores), savings equal over $80K annually. Additional benefits include faster transactions and fewer errors.

Like Diamond Shamrock's hub and spoke configuration, where the "hub" is the larger customer and the "spokes" are its smaller suppliers, many smaller companies end up using EDI over the Internet because it is required by their larger trading partners. For example, in the early 1990s, WalMart asked Cedar Works, a manufacturer of aromatic bird feeders and mailboxes, to start using EDI to take orders and send invoices. In addition to satisfying WalMart and paving the way to potentially use EDI with its other large customers (e.g. Lowe's, Home Depot, Target Stores, and Nature Company), Cedar Works improved customer satisfaction and cash flow.

Just like large-volume companies have migrated away from VANs due to the charge per transaction, much of the EDI transactions are projected to transition to the Internet. General Motors, Ford, and Chrysler in 1996 announced their intentions to move their operations from VANs to Internet service providers. In addition, new Web-based technologies and services like electronic cash may eventually make EDI obsolete. In the meantime, many EDI network operators are establishing gateways for their services to the Internet. For example, General Electric Information Services' (GEIS') TradeWeb is an Internet-based EDI service targeted at America's 2MM small businesses which have traditionally found EDI too expensive to adopt. With TradeWeb, small businesses use four generic forms: 1) purchase order, 2) purchase order acknowledgment, 3) invoice, and 4) functional acknowledgment.

Intranets

An intranet is a network within a company used to share information and conduct business. For large, geographically dispersed companies, it is an excellent way to consolidate volume through a technology solution.

An example of one company which has benefited from using an intranet is National Semiconductor Corporation. It is using its National Supply Catalog (NSC) to obtain more than $12MM worth of material annually. Using the NSC to buy MRO supplies, National Semiconductor automated 80% of its 42K annual purchase orders. This also reduced cycle time from 18 days to often next day delivery, reduced inventory by $1MM, and reduced inventory holding costs by $300K. And, this also brought about a reduction in the cost of processing purchase orders from a range of $75-250 to $3. The procurement staff was also reduced by more than 50%.

In terms of how it works, if you worked at National Semiconductor and wanted to purchase an MRO supply, you would log in to the intranet via a Netscape browser, enter your name and password, and go to the "Home Shopping Page" which would show you the 20 commodities on the system and the approved suppliers for each. After selecting a supplier, you would click through increasingly specific product screens until you got to the product you want to buy. Specifications and prices for the product are indicated. The NSC is highly graphic oriented: "people buy from pictures." Once you know what you want, you would go to the order area and provide the quantity, address, and shipping priority information. Orders are sent via IBM's Advantis electronic mail network.

Internet

In this book's context, commerce on the Internet is primarily about creating electronic connections between trading companies versus tapping into the Internet's more than 50MM users. And, the focus is to primarily reduce costs versus increase revenue. This is particularly true from a purchaser's point of view.

While a number of agencies in the U.S. Government have been using EDI since the 1980s through the Federal Acquisition Network, electronic sourcing (E-sourcing) gained tremendous popularity in the mid-1990s, when General Electric Company launched the GE Trading Process Network (http://www.tpn.geis.com). TPN is a secure, Web-based electronic commerce system that started off connecting GE and its suppliers. Suppliers can use TPN to get engineering specifications, forms, and other information required to respond to inquiries. GE Lighting joined the network as a pilot project in mid-1996, and now works with over 20 international suppliers mainly concentrated in the United Kingdom and Hungary. Since joining the network, GE Lighting cut its average purchasing cycle to seven days, a 50% reduction. Further, they report the openness of the Web results in 10-15% lower prices.

On April 1, 1997, GE spun the Trading Process Network (TPN) into a separate company, TPN Register. Its goal is to license the software and services to other Fortune 500-1000 companies and enable them to reduce the time and cost to purchase primarily MRO supplies and equipment (e.g. office supplies, electrical equipment, industrial equipment). TPN includes TPN Post, designed to collect bids and quotations. In addition, TPN Register is backed by Thomas Publishing Company, a publisher of industrial supply catalogs.

Other forums to bring purchasers and sellers together include:

ProcureNet: http://www.procurenet.com

Manufacturing Net: http://www.manufacturing.net

Industry Net: http://www.industry.net

Purchasing Magazine:
http://www.manufacturing.net/magazine/purchasing/

ProcureNet describes itself as "the Electronic Mall of the future for buyers, sellers, and distributors." It was "designed to help buyers simplify the purchasing process and to help suppliers and distributors avoid the Internet sprawl by grouping them with other suppliers who market to the same customers." Categories of materials it offers range from abrasives; balances, weights, and measurements; bearings; biotechnology; and chemicals; through pumps and compressors; safety products; software; and valves and fittings. Clicking on chemicals suppliers generates a list of suppliers including Acros Organics, Fisher Scientific, LabChem, and SPEX CertPrep.

Manufacturing Net's directory includes views by products and services, suppliers, and trade names. Entering a type of product, for example fasteners, generates a list of suppliers including AGM Container Controls, Avibank Manufacturing, Bollhoff, Hodell-Natco Industries, Lee Autobody Clips & Fasteners, NMB Corporation, and USM Texon Materials.

Industry Net was "established with the primary goal of simplifying the buying and selling process. The On Line Marketplace has formed an interactive, electronic link between manufacturers, distributors, and customers, and helps reduce the costs of doing business." It began in 1990, is headquartered in Pittsburgh, PA and operates out of 18 regional offices across the country. It also offers regional buying guides.

Security is a major concern of buyers and sellers doing business on the Internet. Premenos Corporation partnered with RSA Data Security to ensure transactions conducted over the Internet are secure. Companies doing business via the Secure Socket Layer (SSL) include Amazon.com, Barnes & Noble, Music Boulevard, PC Flowers & Gifts, Ticketmaster, Southwest Airlines, and First Union Bank.

Summary

In this chapter we addressed tactical buying and electronic commerce. This included differences versus sourcing and identifying what is "new" about tactical buying that needs to be considered in supplier selection, the why and how to consolidate volume, centralized versus decentralized procurement, blanket orders, procurement cards, Electronic Data Interchange (EDI), intranets, and the Internet. In light of consolidating volume and reducing the supply base, the benefits of centralized, decentralized, and combination organizations from a procurement standpoint were reviewed. And "work-arounds" or alternatives when an organization is decentralized were provided.

IMPLEMENTATION
AND RESULTS
CHAPTER SEVEN

Introduction

In this chapter we address implementation and results. This includes how to take a balanced approach, have a waved implementation, incorporate change management, and measure performance. The change management framework which consists of four components is reviewed. These components include: navigation (for example, understand stakeholders expectations), leadership (for example, have the procurement initiative be one of the top three to five priorities), ownership (for example, formally identifying and developing change agents), and enablement (for example, training and performance management). In terms of measuring performance, industry-standard examples of procurement measures are provided, the evils of purchase price variance (PPV) discussed, and benchmarks for the electronics and consumer products industries shared. The need to track, analyze, and report results and tie them to incentives is also addressed.

Balanced Approach

In many organizations, contracts are set to expire at the end of the fiscal year, or the end of the calendar year. With the majority of contracts expiring at the same time, there is an inordinate work load before and during strategic sourcing. As a result, either companies maintain staffing to handle this peak (which means higher overhead and underutilization at other times of the year), or the staff is overworked and the quality and results of their work suffers. An illustration of this is shown in Figure 7.1.

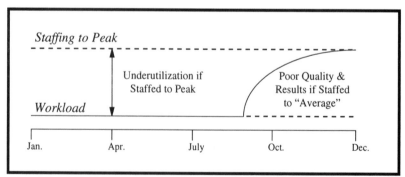

Figure 7.1

In order to stabilize work load and therefore staffing levels, we recommend you spread your contract expirations evenly throughout the year. Assume you are the Purchasing Manager for chemicals and are responsible for twenty-four different types of chemicals. An example of how to spread your expirations, with different contract lengths, over the calendar year is shown in Figure 7.2.

MATERIAL	MATERIAL	MATERIAL	MATERIAL
Chemical U (1 yr.)	Chemical V (1 yr.)	Chemical W (1 yr.)	Chemical X (1 yr.)
Chemical Q (1 yr.)	Chemical R (1 yr.)	Chemical S (1 yr.)	Chemical T (1 yr.)
Chemical M (1 yr.)	Chemical N (1 yr.)	Chemical O (1 yr.)	Chemical P (1 yr.)
Chemical I (2 yrs.)	Chemical J (2 yrs.)	Chemical K (2 yrs.)	Chemical L (1 yr.)
Chemical E (2 yrs.)	Chemical F (2 yrs.)	Chemical G (2 yrs.)	Chemical H (2 yrs.)
Chemical A (3 yrs.)	Chemical B (3 yrs.)	Chemical C (4 yrs.)	Chemical D (5 yrs.)
CONTRACT EXPIRES	CONTRACT EXPIRES	CONTRACT EXPIRES	CONTRACT EXPIRES
January – U & A	April – V & B	July – W & C	October – X & D
February – Q & E	May – R & F	August – S & G	November – T & H
March – M & I	June – N & J	September – O & K	December – P & L

Figure 7.2

In terms of a migration plan from what you are doing now to a balanced approach, follow the steps below:

1) List all the materials you are responsible for, along with their type of agreement (e.g. spot, blanket order, contract, etc.) and length of agreement (e.g. 1 year, 2 years, etc.).

2) Build a spreadsheet with twelve columns, and label each column with a month (e.g. first column January, second column February, etc.).

3) List your materials in the column which corresponds with when the agreement expires, with an indication of the length of the agreement in parentheses (e.g. 1 yr.). Spot purchases should be listed in every column. Blanket orders should be listed when the blanket order expires. The result is your "As Is" work load.

4) Build another spreadsheet with twelve columns labeled with months.

5) Using Figure 7.2 as an example, spread your materials over the columns to get a balance in both length of agreement and number of materials in each month. Start with the longest agreements first, and do spot purchases last. The result is your straw model "To Be" work load.

6) To this point, the above approach assumes all materials take about the same amount of time. Look over your straw model "To Be" work load and highlight in yellow the three materials which take considerably more than average time. Also, highlight in some other color the three materials which take considerably less than average time. Adjust your straw model "To Be" work load to make sure the top three materials are each in separate quarters, separated by at least two months. Also, make adjustments to pair the bottom three materials with the top three materials. The result is your "final" "To Be" work load.

7) As your materials come due, write the new expiration date to correspond to your "To Be" work load plan, even if that means the agreement is

for an "odd" number of months (e.g. 7, 16, 23, etc.). Continue to work your plan over time, and you will have eventually migrated from your "As Is" work load to your "To Be" work load. Depending on the length of your current contracts, this process may take several years.

Waved Implementation

Similar to the plan to migrate your purchasing patterns to a more balanced approach, you should develop a plan of attack to migrate more toward strategic sourcing. For example, Mead Johnson Nutritionals, a division of Bristol-Myers Squibb, took a three-waved approach to strategic sourcing with a goal of cost reduction. The waves, timing, and expected benefits they identified are shown in Figure 7.3.

Change Management

All of the things we have addressed in this book: mission and vision, strategic sourcing imperative, situation analysis, supply strategy, strategic sourcing, tactical buying and electronic commerce, and taking a balanced approach, represent change of some kind. Managing change is critical before, during, and after implementation in order to get the desired results.

Andersen Consulting defines change management as "the discipline that ensures organizations and employees meet new and existing performance targets rapidly and effectively." It is based on two concepts:

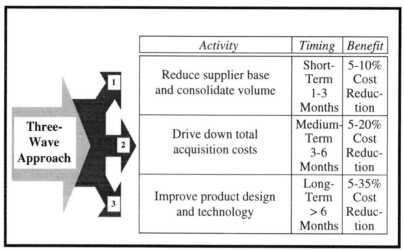

	Activity	Timing	Benefit
1	Reduce supplier base and consolidate volume	Short-Term 1-3 Months	5-10% Cost Reduc-tion
2	Drive down total acquisition costs	Medium-Term 3-6 Months	5-20% Cost Reduc-tion
3	Improve product design and technology	Long-Term > 6 Months	5-35% Cost Reduc-tion

Figure 7.3 – Reprinted with permission from the publisher, the National Association of Purchasing Management, "The Synergy of Strategic Sourcing," by Jon Ricker, C.P.M., CPIM, Purchasing Today®, *Volume 8, Number 5, pp. 42-44.*

1) Human performance is at the core of business performance.
2) It is possible to optimize an organization's revenue and profit delivery during change.

There are four outcomes sought from change management:

1) Employees deliver performance targets on time, on budget.
2) Stakeholders remain loyal; new stakeholders are attracted and provide support.
3) Risks associated with change are eliminated or reduced.
4) The organization is better able to change rapidly and effectively in the future.

Before embarking on this change journey, there are some questions that should be asked (and answered) regarding an organization's ability to successfully make the journey. Keeping the types of changes we have addressed in the book in mind, write answers to the sample questions below regarding your organization's ability to make this journey.

- **Are the organization culture, structure, and human resource investments aligned with the strategic goals?**

  _____

  _____

  _____

- **Can we create competitive advantage or lower risk cost effectively by altering the skills and behaviors of the employees?**

  _____

  _____

  _____

- **Is the executive team seen as effectively leading the change initiative? How important is this to internal and external stakeholder support?**

  _____

  _____

  _____

- **What is the reality check from the average employee? What are the real issues and barri-**

ers to change? How does this view differ among employee groups?

_____

_____

_____

• Are the change initiatives properly planned, scoped, and paced so that its businesses can meet their performance targets, and its investments in change are targeted at the areas where greatest benefit can be reaped?

_____

_____

_____

• How important are external stakeholders to the organization's ability to achieve its change goals? What actions do we need them (e.g. suppliers) to take?

_____

_____

_____

• Does the organization demonstrate a human capital mindset - one that focuses on enhancing value and investing in its human assets? How can this be improved?

_____

_____

_____

- Does the organization have the capacity to undertake the proposed changes? What needs to be done to enhance this capacity?

_____

_____

_____

- Who "loses" if the change does not happen?

_____

_____

_____

The Journey Management Framework shown in Figure 7.4 provides a roadmap of four areas to be addressed when defining a course of action for any change journey. This roadmap is to ensure superior human and organization performance. Together, these four areas encompass the demand for, and supply of, change, and consider change at both the micro (personal, individual) and macro (organizational) levels.

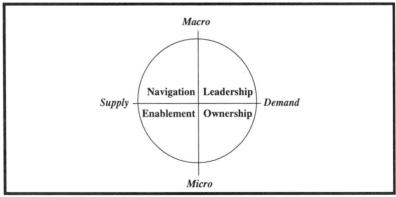

Figure 7.4

A description of each of these four areas to be addressed when defining a course of action are noted below.

Navigation – Navigation ensures change is well planned, directed, measured, led, and managed. Effective change navigation predicts and minimizes the negative outcomes of change, such as productivity declines and stakeholder conflicts. The result is greater assurance that key performance targets will be met.

Leadership – Leadership delivers effective communication, role modeling, and problem-solving by the organization's executives and their top teams, as well as by middle managers and supervisors as change initiatives cascade through the organization. Effective leadership helps ensure internal and external stakeholders remain committed to the organization and its change goals.

Ownership – Ownership helps deliver a culture of individual accountability and daily problem-solving. This is accomplished by building widespread acceptance and personal responsibility for change so the organization's change goals and action plans are "owned" by all individuals responsible for delivering them.

Enablement – Enablement ensures employees are able to take action and meet specific performance targets. Given that many variables influence employees' ability to perform, enablement touches on many areas. Some of these areas include: knowledge and skill development, human resource policies and support structures, and organization and job design.

As noted above, change management is focused on ensuring that organizations and employees meet new and existing performance targets rapidly and effectively. Given that context, we now turn our attention to performance measurement.

Performance Measurement

In this section we address performance measurement in general and procurement measurement in detail. When it comes to performance measurement, some lessons learned by other companies in terms of "what works" and "what doesn't work" are recapped in Figure 7.5.

What Has Worked	*Mistakes To Avoid*

• KPMs meet SMART criteria:
  • Specific
  • Measurable
  • Attainable
  • Result Oriented
  • Time Bound
• KPMs are accomplishment based
• Limited number of measures
• Level of precision necessary
• Use families of measures
• Develop team-oriented measures
• Constantly raise expectations/goals
• Revise as needed
	• Measure the wrong things right
	• Let the process get sidetracked; do not demonstrate resolve through behavior
	• Let cross-functional conflicts get out of control
	• Do not have somebody accountable
	• Allow some people or areas to be "exempt"
	• Do not track results and look for and analyze trends
	• Results are not visible in "scorecards" or on "performance boards"
	• Executives don't focus on the KPMs

Figure 7.5

In addition, when establishing key performance measures (KPMs), it is important to remember three critical things:

1) **Do not mistake data for information.**

2) You are what you measure.

3) What gets measured gets managed.

How data is collected is important. Data collection considerations include a sampling plan, the collection process, resources utilized, capable and validated measurement systems, and types of data. Data is one of two types: 1) attribute (yes/no, pass/fail, in/out, present/absent); or 2) variable (actual measure, which varies).

After data is collected, tracking results and looking for and analyzing trends are often overlooked. A basic method to do this is to plot measurement results over time. A more sophisticated method to do this is to develop a control chart. Steps for developing a control chart are listed below:

1) Develop a sampling plan; collect data
2) Chart data against value (Y axis) and time (X axis)
3) Determine average ($\bar{x}$); chart
4) Calculate upper control limit (UCL) and lower control limit (LCL); chart
5) Look for special causes; analyze; develop next steps to address
6) Look for trends
7) Ensure statistical significance in data collection, control limits, special causes, and trends

While how to calculate upper and lower control limits and determining statistical significance is beyond the scope of this book, Figure 7.6 is a generic (non-scaled) example of what a control chart looks like.

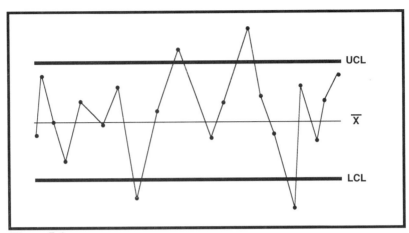

Figure 7.6

In this example, the points above and below the control limits would warrant special cause investigation. Plotting measurement results over time and control charting are only two of many ways to start root cause analysis. Other tools which can be used for root cause analysis include flow charts, brainstorming, Pareto charts, histograms, and cause and effect (fishbone) diagrams. Of these, Pareto charts are often the most powerful to establish priorities and allocate resources. Steps for developing a Pareto chart are listed below:

1) Develop a sampling plan; collect data.

2) Identify causes.

3) Determine frequency of causes.

4) Construct a Pareto chart - number of occurrences (Y axis) and causes in decreasing order of frequency (X axis).

5) Analyze Pareto chart; determine top priorities.

6) Develop next steps; implement.

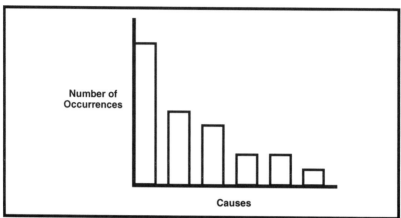

Figure 7.7

Figure 7.7 is a generic example of what a Pareto chart looks like.

Some typical barriers to root cause solutions to look out for, which are often seen as resistance to change, include:

"We've always done it that way."

"It takes too much time."

"My mind is already made up."

"They wouldn't let us do it."

"Don't want to know; if I know, I might have to act."

"It costs too much."

"Why bother?"

"Fix the symptoms."

"If it's not broken, don't fix it."

"If it's close enough, it's good enough."

In terms of procurement measurement, there are many different measures which can be utilized. Sample

Measure	Electronics	Consumer Products
Defect-free performance	99%	98.5%
Inventory turns	10.5	7.3
Supplier base concentration	20:75	20:80
Purchase volume per employee	$7.1MM	$14.1MM
Purchase value as % of revenue	34%	48%
On-time delivery performance	94.7%	97.5%
Order cycle time	2 days	2 days
Purchase cycle time	28 days	3 days
% of suppliers formally evaluated	80%	> 90%
% of orders transmitted over EDI	> 40%	6.5%
Frequency of stockouts	1.5%	2%
Utilization of blanket orders	20%	N.A.
Requisition cycle time	< 60 min.	< 10 min.
Requisition approval cycle time	30-120 min.	N.A.
Purch. order placement cycle time	.4-.5 days	1 day
Purchase order approval cycle time	.4-.5 days	1 day
Receiving cycle time	< 1 hr.	< 1 hr.
Inspection cycle time	4-8 hrs.	2-36 hrs.

Figure 7.8 – Sources: Andersen Consulting commissioned study (March 1994) & Center for Advanced Purchasing Studies (CAPS).

measures, along with benchmarks for the electronics and consumer products industries, are shown in Figure 7.8.

An example of performance measures used by a food consumer products company at one of its facilities focused on rapid replenishment is shown in Figure 7.9. Rapid replenishment means having accurate system inventory, a continuous material replenishment process, efficient material storage, and an improvement program with suppliers to reduce lead times. It assures the availability of raw material for manufacturing by having the ability to order and quickly receive line-ready material from suppliers.

One measure noticeably absent from these lists is purchase price variance (PPV). Purchase price variance

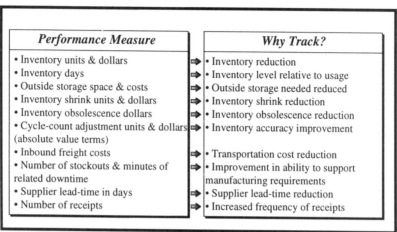

Performance Measure		Why Track?
• Inventory units & dollars	⇒	• Inventory reduction
• Inventory days	⇒	• Inventory level relative to usage
• Outside storage space & costs	⇒	• Outside storage needed reduced
• Inventory shrink units & dollars	⇒	• Inventory shrink reduction
• Inventory obsolescence dollars	⇒	• Inventory obsolescence reduction
• Cycle-count adjustment units & dollars (absolute value terms)	⇒	• Inventory accuracy improvement
• Inbound freight costs	⇒	• Transportation cost reduction
• Number of stockouts & minutes of related downtime	⇒	• Improvement in ability to support manufacturing requirements
• Supplier lead-time in days	⇒	• Supplier lead-time reduction
• Number of receipts	⇒	• Increased frequency of receipts

Figure 7.9

is the difference in price between what was paid to the supplier and the standard cost of that item. It is thought to have been derived from the railroad industry in the early 1900s, and no longer serves its purpose, and it is often abused by procurement professionals and executives alike.

Specifically, a common practice in many companies today is for procurement professionals to forecast material prices then measure "savings" as the difference between actual prices versus forecasted prices. Forecasts are usually very conservative, and often inflated, to ensure actual prices are at, or below, forecast, thus meeting goal. This is really "funny money," which only results in actual costs lower than forecasted costs. This "windfall" often becomes something executives count on and use as a "slush fund" of sorts for all kinds of unbudgeted and unanticipated projects and expenses.

If you use PPV, we recommend eliminating it. The reasoning is you could have great PPV, but have material costs higher than the prior period (e.g. last year). While forecasting is obviously important, procurement should be measured by actual total costs and results.

Consider the key performance indicators currently used for procurement in your company. Write those down the left column below. In the right column, indicate KPMs you think would add more value in the future.

"As Is" KPMs   **"To Be" KPMs**

_____   _____

_____   _____

_____   _____

_____   _____

_____   _____

_____   _____

As seen from PPV, tying results to performance incentives needs to be done carefully, i.e., in a way that you get the desired behaviors you want. It is important to tie incentives to the "new" performance measures. If you reward people the "old" way they are going to behave the "old" way. You want them to behave the "new" way. A summary of financial performance measures used to determine compensation of top executives in 1993 is shown in Figure 7.10.

This brings us full circle back to the strategic sourcing imperative. As noted in Chapter Two, a 1% reduction in cost of goods sold (COGS) delivers the same margin

Performance Measures *	Annual Compensation (% of cos.)	Long-Term Compensation (% of cos.)
Return on equity	37	32
Net income	32	15
Earnings per share	29	26
Stock price appreciation	27	52
Pre-tax profit	23	16
Revenue	20	12
Return on assets	19	14
Operating profit	16	7
Cost reduction	13	3
Cash flow	12	9
Return on capital employed	6	5
Working capital	5	5
Inventory	2	3
Economic value added **	1	0
Receivables	1	0
Price competition	0	3

* Companies may use more than one to set compensation.
** The total cost of the company's or business unit's capital.
Variable pay is based on year-to-year improvements.

Figure 7.10 – Source: "Top Executive Pay for Performance," The Conference Board, Report No. 1113-95-RR, 1995.

lift as 12-18% sales growth. Tying new key performance measures to incentives will cause new behaviors and drive business results. While the example we provided regarding incentives was for top executives, as performance measures are cascaded through an organization, incentives at every level need to be reviewed and revised accordingly. This is particularly true for procurement professionals and individuals engaged in cross-functional sourcing teams.

Summary

In this chapter we addressed implementation and results. This included how to take a balanced approach, have a waved implementation, incorporate change management, and measure performance. A change management framework consisting of four components was reviewed: 1) navigation, 2) leadership, 3) ownership, and 4) enablement. In terms of measuring performance, industry-standard examples of procurement measures were provided, the evils of purchase price variance (PPV) discussed, and benchmarks for the electronics and consumer products industries shared. The need to track, analyze, and report results and tie them to incentives was also addressed.

ADDITIONAL PURCHASING RESOURCES

FROM PT PUBLICATIONS, INC.

3109 45th Street, Suite 100
West Palm Beach, FL 33407-1915
1-800-547-4326

THE PURCHASING ENCYCLOPEDIA

Just-In-Time Purchasing: In Pursuit of Excellence $29.95
    Peter L. Grieco, Jr., Michael W. Gozzo
    & Jerry W. Claunch

Glossary of Key Purchasing Terms, Acronyms, *and Formulas* PT Publications	$14.95
Supplier Certification II: A Handbook for *Achieving Excellence through Continuous Improvement* Peter L. Grieco, Jr.	$49.95
World Class: Measuring Its Achievement Peter L. Grieco, Jr.	$39.95
Purchasing Performance Measurements: A Roadmap *For Excellence* Mel Pilachowski	$12.95
The World Of Negotiations: Never Being a Loser Peter L. Grieco, Jr. and Paul G. Hine	$39.95
How To Conduct Supplier Surveys and Audits Janet L. Przirembel	$14.95
Supply Management Toolbox: How to Manage *Your Suppliers* Peter L. Grieco, Jr.	$26.95
Purchasing Capital Equipment Wayne L. Douchkoff	$14.95
Power Purchasing: Supply Management in *in the 21st Century* Peter L. Grieco, Jr. and Carl R. Cooper	$39.95
Global Sourcing Lee Krotseng	$14.95
Purchasing Contract Law, UCC, and Patents Mark Grieco	$14.95
EDI Purchasing: The Electronic Gateway *to the Future* Steven Marks	$14.95
Leasing Smart Craig A. Melby and Jane Utzman	$14.95
MRO Purchasing Peter L. Grieco, Jr.	$14.95
Purchasing Transportation Charles L. Perry	$14.95

The Complete Guide to Contracts Management For $18.95
    Facilities Services
    John P. Mahoney and Linda S. Keckler

PURCHASING VIDEO EDUCATION SERIES

Supplier Certification The Path to Excellence
    Tape 1: Why Supplier Certification? $395.00
    Tape 2: Quality at the Supplier $395.00
    Tape 3: How to Select a Supplier $395.00
    Tape 4: Supplier Surveys and Audits $395.00
    Tape 5: Supplier Quality Agreements $395.00
    Tape 6: Supplier Ratings $395.00
    Tape 7: Phases of Supplier Certification $395.00
    Tape 8: Implementing a Supplier Cert. Program $395.00
    Tape 9: Evaluating Your Supplier Cert. Program $395.00

    Complete Nine Tape Series $1,995.00

PURCHASING AUDIO TAPES

The World of Negotiations: How to Win Every Time $39.95

PURCHASING SOFTWARE

Supplier Survey and Audit Software $395.00
    Developed by Professionals For Technology, Inc.

ADDITIONAL PROFESSIONAL TEXTBOOKS

Failure Modes and Effects Analysis: Predicting $39.95
    and Preventing Problems Before They Occur
    Paul Palady
Made In America: The Total Business Concept $29.95
    Peter L. Grieco, Jr. and Michael W. Gozzo

Reengineering Through Cycle Time Management $39.95
    Wayne L. Douchkoff and Thomas E. Petroski

Behind Bars: Bar Coding Principles and Applications $39.95
    Peter L. Grieco, Jr., Michael W. Gozzo and C.J. Long

People Empowerment: Achieving Success from Involvement $39.95
    Michael W. Gozzo and Wayne L. Douchkoff

Activity Based Costing: The Key to World Class Performance $18.00
    Peter L. Grieco, Jr. and Mel Pilachowski

Index

W

Waste 15-17
Waved implementation 127-128
Weaknesses 57, 58, 59
Weighting guidelines 87, 102
Work-arounds 110-111
Work load 121-127

X

X.12 standards 116